PROGRESSIVE
>>>>> Police
Supervision

A Simple & Effective
Approach for Managing
a Police Agency

JODY KASPER

Looseleaf
Law Publications, Inc.

43-08 162nd Street
Flushing, NY 11358
www.LooseleafLaw.com
800-647-5547

Library of Congress Cataloging-in-Publication Data

Kasper, Jody.
    Progressive police supervision : a simple and effective approach for managing a police agency / Jody Kasper.
       p. cm.
    Includes bibliographical references and index.
    ISBN 978-1-60885-022-8
 1. Police administration--United States. 2. Law enforcement--United States. 3. Community policing--United States. 4. Police-community relations--United States. I. Title.
 HV8141.K37 2010
 363.2068--dc22

2010038820

Cover by *Sans Serif*, Saline, Michigan

Table of Contents

About the Author i

Introduction iii

Chapter 1
A Brief History of Policing in America 1
    Robert Peel's London Metropolitan Police 1
    Special Focus 1.1: Peel's Principles 2
    The Political Era (1830 – 1940) 3
    The Reform Era (1930 – 1970) 4
    Police Community Relations 5
    Precursors to the Community Policing Era 5
    Community Policing Era (1980 – 2001?) 7
    A New Era 8

Chapter 2
Community Policing: What Is It ? 11
    Special Focus 2.1:
        Traditional Policing versus Community Policing . 12
    Community Policing Defined 12
    Identifying the Stakeholders 13
    Key Elements of Community Policing 14

Chapter 3
The End of Community Policing 19
    Identifying the Problems with Community Policing .. 19
    Special Focus 3.1: The Challenges of Implementing
        Community Policing at the Northampton,
        Massachusetts Police Department 24

Chapter 4
Today's Police Departments: Facing New Challenges . 31
    Terrorism 32
    Interoperability 32
    Funding 33
    Community Expectations 33
    Technology 33
    Media 34
    Professionalism/Accountability 35
    Education 35

Chapter 5
Keeping Focused: Identifying the Goals of
   Today's Police Department 37
      Mission Statements 37
      Special Focus 5.1: Sample Mission Statements 37
      Identifying Specific Goals 39
      Special Focus 5.2: Recruiting Strategies 43

Chapter 6
The Millennials: Understanding the Next Generation 49
      Defining the Millennial Generation 49
      Millennial Characteristics 50
      Millennial Expectations—Advancement 51
      Millennial Expectations—Supervisory Contact 52
      Millennial Expectations—Fairness 53
      Millennial Expectations—Community/Global
         Perspective 54

Chapter 7
Supervising in a New Era 57
      Manager versus Leader 57
      Contemporary Leadership Styles 57
      Reengineering the Corporation 59
      Management by Walking Around 60
      Total Quality Management 60
      Special Focus 7.1: Example: Total Quality Management
         Put into Practice 62
      The Peter Principle 64
      The Dilbert Principle 65
      Characteristics of a Good Supervisor 65
      Special Focus 7.2: Selecting the Best: How to Select
         Personnel for Promotion and Special Assignment 67

Chapter 8
The Foundation of Every Police Department 71
      Administrative Duties 71
      Special Focus 8.1: Administrative Duties: East Brunswick,
         New Jersey Police Department 72
      Accreditation 73
      Special Focus 8.2: Becoming Accredited:
         A Five-Step Process 75
      Minimum Hiring Standards—Education 76
      Recruitment and Hiring 80

Police Training 82

Personnel Evaluations 84

New Technology 86

Chapter 9
Police-Media Relations: Actively Shaping the Public's
  Image of the Police 91

Defining Media 91

  Developing Positive Working Relationships with the
  Members of the Media 92

Self-promotion 92

  Special Focus 9.1: Generating Positive Media
  Coverage: The 2008 and 2009 Citizen Police
  Academies Held by the Northampton, Massachusetts
  Police Department 93

Police Website 94

"Ask a Cop" Programs 95

Public Service Announcements 95

Creating Media Materials 95

Contributions to the Police Image 95

Chapter 10
Patrol: Emphasizing Progressive Strategies 97

Key Components of Effective Patrol Methods 97

  Proactive Approach 97

  Special Focus 10.1: Sheriff's Theft Offense
    Prosecution Program (STOPP), Fairfield County,
    Ohio, Sheriff's Office 98

  Geographic Patrol Assignment 99

  Accountability 100

  Community Partnerships and Collaboration 100

  Special Focus 10.2: Hampshire County Sexual
    Assault Response Team (SART) 101

Forms of Patrol 103

  Cruiser Patrol 103

  Bicycle Patrol 104

  Foot Patrol 104

Park and Walk Programs 105

Chapter 11
Community Outreach: Proven Strategies That Work 107

Citizen Police Academy 107

Special Focus 11.1: Improving the Police Image: Anonymous Surveys Collected from Participants of a 2009 Citizen Police Academy 108
Ride-along Programs 110
Park and Walk 110
Neighborhood Watch 111
Special Focus 11.2: Neighborhood Watch, Farmington Hills, Michigan Police Department 111
Self-defense Programs 113
Police Week/Police Day 113
Interns 113
Other Outreach Activities 114
Citizen Surveys 114

Chapter 12
Schools: Working Together **117**
Communication and Collaboration: The School-Police Connection 118
Incident Training and Drills: Preparing for the Worst119
Building Safety and Security: Physical Tactics 119
Special Assignments: Officers Working Inside Schools120
Special Focus 12.1: Bullying 122
Educational Programming: Prevention through Understanding 125
Proven Success 125

Chapter 13
Implementing Change: Have No Fear **129**
A History of Resisting Change 130
Successfully Implementing Change 130
Accept that Change Is Inevitable 130
Give Advanced Warning 131
Explain the Reason for the Change 131
Involve Employees in the Change Process 131
Provide Orientation and Training (if necessary) 132
Prepare to Reassess and Improve 133
Conclusion 134

Index **137**

Jody Kasper is a Patrol Sergeant with the Northampton, Massachusetts Police Department. For more than a decade, she has worked in a variety of positions within that agency, including assignments to the Bicycle Patrol Unit, Field Training and Evaluation Program, Detective Bureau and finally as a Sergeant.

In addition to her patrol duties she manages the agency's website, coordinates the Citizen Police Academy, serves as the department's Community Services Liaison and runs the Ride-along Program.

Outside of her work with NPD she is an adjunct professor at Elms College where she teaches classes in Violence, Criminal Justice and Forensic Psychology. She is also an instructor for the Municipal Police Training Committee. She has written articles for *Law and Order Magazine, Police Recruit* and *The Police Chief.*

Sgt. Kasper has a dual Bachelor's degree in Criminal Justice and in Psychology. She also has Master's degrees in Criminal Justice and Public Administration.

Police administrators and street-level supervisors are facing new challenges in a changing world. With tightened budgets, expanded duties, new community fears and advances in technology, administrators are leading departments that are unlike any others before them. In addition to these external changes, the types of employees that comprise the bulk of patrol officers are a new generation of people, with different values and who are responsive to different supervisory strategies.

Community policing has been around for over 30 years. Citizens, police administrators, researchers and politicians have latched onto the concept. The name conjures up images of people working together, solving problems and the disappearance of the divide that once existed between the people and their police. There has been such a commitment to this concept that theorists have labeled the past three decades the Community Policing Era.

It was reasonable and necessary that the field of policing in America entered into this new Era. Historically, policing transformed from loosely organized groups of private citizens into more structured and formal agencies with sworn personnel. However, once established, these formal agencies went through many phases that characterized the state of policing at that time. The Political Era represented a time when inexperienced officers were committed to the politicians who appointed them. Then the Reform Era brought professionalism and accountability but removed officers from their communities so that they were no longer connected to the people who they served. The Community Policing Era was the beginning of a national commitment to bridge this gap between the people and their police. It is a brilliant idea and many of its components are completely applicable to policing today.

Although many police officers and administrators claim that they practice community policing, a closer look at their organizational structure and everyday operations are not reflective of a true community policing agency. Police departments have been unable to fully transition to fit the intended philosophy. Change takes time and the original theorists behind community policing estimated that most agencies would take 10 – 15 years to make the transition. So over 30 years later, why have so many police departments been unable to fully adopt this seemingly simple idea?

Police departments' inability to convert to community policing should lead criminal justice researchers and progressive administrators to re-evaluate the entire concept. In an ideal world, with ideal police administrators, ideal police recruits and a steady and ample financial support system, community policing would have a shot. Unfortunately, most police agencies do not exist in this utopia and administrators are forced to work with what they have.

This book challenges the universal application of true community policing philosophy to every department in America. Instead, it suggests that we have moved beyond this age to a new era. While there are tangible strategies and programs that today's police administrator can integrate into current police practices imbedded within community policing, it is time to move away from this thinking and to embrace a new era of police leadership and management.

The ideas presented in this book are tangible, creative, progressive and consistent with current police practices. They provide police administrators and street-level managers with the ideas necessary to attract and retain officers. This is done by identifying the needs of the Millennial workforce and of today's citizens. Once these needs are recognized, administrators can steer their individual agencies toward meeting them. Most of these strategies involve providing personnel with new challenges and opportunities that will keep them motivated, improve morale and foster positive public relations. These outcomes will ultimately improve the quality of life in their respective communities, enhance working environments for officers and reduce crime.

After the events of September 11, 2001, the atmosphere of the entire nation changed and with that the expectations and focus of police departments were forced to shift dramatically away from community policing. In this new, yet undefined era, there is more focus on global activity, homeland security, terrorism and the ability of police departments and other emergency personnel to respond to large-scale critical incidents effectively.

This new focus has resulted in a shift of federal and state funding from community oriented programs and positions to military efforts and law enforcement activities that are reflective of the nation's new concerns.

As the country operates in this new era, police administrators are forced to re-evaluate their overall missions, identified goals and the needs of the community as a whole. It is evident that community policing has significantly improved police-public relations. A comparative analysis through the decades would reveal this enhanced relationship. However, in this new era with a focus on homeland security, terrorism and fear, it is imperative that administrators move away from community policing by extracting the successful strategies that it provided and applying them to current practices.

Community policing is a philosophy that has proven too challenging for many departments to adopt in its purest form. As the country transitions away from this era, it is important to move from an idealistic application of the original theory to a more practical supervisory approach that integrates the effective strategies and goals of traditional community policing into the everyday practices of today's police officer.

This book is intended for law enforcement practitioners serving in leadership roles. It explains the state of policing today, encourages an assessment of current needs of individual agencies and of entire communities, examines the characteristics and needs of the incoming workforce of the Millennial generation, explains contemporary leadership concepts, assesses progressive administrative roles and opportunities, suggests a proactive media strategy, identifies specific progressive patrol strategies, encourages effective community outreach plans, articulates a clear and concise plan for school-police partnerships and explains the best strategies for implementing change. It is an overview of what progressive and forward-thinking administrators can do to keep their departments on the cutting edge, despite limited financial resources and expanded responsibilities.

> *It is only for ease of reading that the masculine or feminine pronoun is selectively used herein.*

A brief overview of the history of law enforcement is useful to provide insight into exactly how American police departments have developed into what they are today. It is necessary to trace this evolutionary path so that one can best understand the concept of community policing, why it was first introduced and how we have moved beyond it.

Early policing history involves the use of private citizens working as individuals or in small groups. They engaged in activities, such as nighttime watches, that laid the foundation for modern patrol methods. For the purposes of this book, however, it is only necessary to include a brief and more recent account of policing history.

Robert Peel's London Metropolitan Police

Modern police agencies are rooted in Sir Robert Peel's London Metropolitan Police Department established in 1829. Peel firmly believed in accountability, honesty and trust. In his *Principles of Law Enforcement*, he detailed specific ideologies that, he believed, should form the cornerstone of a successful and professional police organization *(Special Focus 1.1)*. Within his principles he wrote, "The police are the public and the public are the police *(Carter, 2002, p. 5)*." As this statement illustrates, Peel recognized that there should be no division between the people and their police. His newly developed police unit was successful at reducing crime and similar police agencies continued to develop around the United Kingdom.

American policing has its roots in Peelian law enforcement agencies in England. Its history involves constables, sheriffs and the vigilante justice system that occurred as the country expanded westward. In the aftermath of Peel's successful Metropolitan Police, organized police agencies began to develop in the United States in the mid-1800s in cities such as Philadelphia (1833), Boston (1838) and New York City (1844). Over time officers began wearing uniforms, detective bureaus were formed and officers patrolled on horseback and on foot. Essentially, departments began to organize and function in a manner reflective of modern day police agencies.

Special Focus 1.1: Peel's Principles

Robert Peel created his Principles of Law Enforcement in 1829. These ideologies provided the basis for the London Metropolitan Police Department, which, in turn, served as the foundation for much of modern day policing in the United States. Many of the essential components of community policing can be found within Peel's early writing.

1. The basic mission for which the police exist is to prevent crime and disorder as an alternative to the repression of crime and disorder by military force and severity of legal punishment.

2. The ability of the police to perform their duties is dependent on public approval of police existence, actions, behavior, and the ability of the police to secure and maintain public respect.

3. The police must secure the willing cooperation of the public in voluntary observance of the law to be able to secure and maintain public respect.

4. The degree of cooperation of the public that can be secured diminishes, proportionately, the necessity for the use of physical force and compulsion in achieving police objectives.

5. The police seek and preserve public favor, not by catering to public opinion, but by constantly demonstrating absolutely impartial service to the law, in complete independence of policy, and without regard to the justice or injustice of the substance of individual laws; by ready offering of individual service and

friendship to all members of the society, without regard to their race or social standing; by ready exercise of courtesy and friendly good humor; and by ready offering of individual sacrifice in protecting and preserving life.

6. The police should use physical force to the extent necessary to secure observance of the law or to restore order only when the exercise of persuasion, advice, and warning is found to be insufficient to achieve police objectives; and police should use only the minimum degree of physical force that is necessary on any particular occasion for achieving a police objective.

7. The police at all times should maintain a relationship with the public that gives reality to the historic tradition that the police are the public and the public are the police; the police are the only members of the public who are paid to give full-time attention to the duties that are incumbent on every citizen in the interest of the community welfare.

8. The police should always direct their actions toward their functions and never appear to usurp the powers of the judiciary by avenging individuals or the state, or authoritatively judging guilt or punishing the guilty.

9. The test of police efficiency is the absence of crime and disorder, not the visible evidence of police action in dealing with them.

Sources:
Carter, David L. (2002). *The Police and the Community*, 7th ed. Upper Saddle River, NJ: Pearson Education, Inc. p. 5.

The Political Era (1830 – 1940)

As departments developed so did widespread corruption. In the world of law enforcement the period between 1830 and 1940 is referred to as The Political Era. During these decades police agencies were driven by political forces. Politicians appointed administrators and officers and all were indebted to those who hired them. Outside of obvious favoritism and corruption, police employees constantly changed as new politicians were elected and could remove and replace employees at will. This resulted in a plethora of inexperienced and incompetent people comprising the majority of most police departments. The widespread political patronage, corruption and incompetence ultimately sparked a transition to the Reform Era.

The Reform Era (1930 – 1970)

The Reform Era emphasized professionalism, rigid organizational structure with centralized authority, limited discretion and accountability. It was determined that police officers should be honest, impartial and well managed. The focus shifted to consistent management that was built on the shoulders of experienced and professional police leaders. There was a clearly defined hierarchy and established lines of authority and specialization. There was further emphasis on the development of departmental policies and procedures. The overall goals were to eliminate the close affiliations that officers had with community members in an effort to reduce the likelihood of favoritism and to professionalize policing.

Also, during this time of reform were several technical developments that further detached police officers from their communities. The rise of the automobile removed officers from their walking beats and put them into cars. Advances in portable radio systems allowed officers to answer calls from their cars without having to walk to call boxes on street corners. Although most would argue that these developments greatly enhanced police departments, they also had the unintended negative consequence of reducing personal contacts and separating the police from the people.

The structural changes within police departments and the technological changes that occurred within the Reform Era substantially affected the public's perception of law enforcement. The police had done so well removing themselves from their communities and breaking their individual ties with community members that there was a deep line drawn in the sand. People no longer felt that the police represented them. There was a lack of empathy on both parts and a very clear "us versus them" mentality developed.

Police Community Relations

During the 1950s the early beginning of Community Policing can be found. It was during this time that Michigan State University initiated the Police Community Relations (PCR) movement *(Radelet, 1980)*. The overall goal of this movement was to ease the tension between the police and the people by educating community members about law enforcement. Initially, the movement failed to incorporate training the police about the communities that they served, but this element was introduced as the need became apparent. Early on the PCR movement focused on minority populations, but that too changed as PCR programs became more popular.

By the 1970s, the PCR movement had caught on and many police agencies had adopted similar programs. The limitation of PCR is that it focused solely on relationships and not on problem-solving and working with community members. While PCR certainly improved community relationships and planted the seed for community policing, discord between police departments and the communities that they served was still present.

Precursors to the Community Policing Era

This divide between the people and the police was illustrated during the 1960s and 1970s: the Civil Rights movement was at its peak; the United States was at war with Vietnam. Both events fueled civil unrest in the form of riots, marches, demonstrations and protests. Multiple cases of excessive use of force occurred nationwide and the media began to bring widespread attention to this issue. Generally, the police appeared to be aloof and detached and there was a lack of empathy between the people and the police and a feeling of distrust that went both ways.

Images of police officers engaged in physical conflicts with American citizens filled the media. The public began to see the police as representatives of the U.S. government and their war policies. A climate of anti-authoritarianism and "fight the power" swept across the nation.

Another interesting component of this time was the complete lack of attention that victims received from the criminal justice system. Individuals who were the victims of crimes were involved early on in investigations but were quickly abandoned as investigations progressed and cases were brought to court. There were limited resources available for victims and little recognition of "special victims" such as those who had been sexually assaulted or who were involved in intimate family violence. Issues such as domestic violence and marital rape were foreign terms and didn't gain recognition within the criminal court system until the 1970s and 1980s. In 1979, Leonore Walker's book, *Battered Woman's Syndrome*, introduced the concept of the cycle of violence in domestic relationships. Prior to recognition of these issues and the importance of relationships with victims and witnesses, the police maintained a narrow focus of crime-fighting and arrest. Victims and others involved in crimes were rarely considered.

During this time one of the most important studies in police patrol strategies ever conducted took place in Kansas City. The Kansas City Preventative Patrol Experiment (KCPPE) took place in 1972 *(Kelling, 1974)*. The city was divided into 15 separate areas. Three different patrol strategies were employed and they were equally divided among the 15 beat areas. One strategy used reactive policing, where police units did not randomly patrol, but instead responded only to calls for service. A second strategy doubled the amount of cars that randomly patrol their assigned areas. The third strategy kept patrol tactics exactly as they had been so that the researchers would have control areas to compare to the test regions. The intent of the study was to determine if the varied styles of patrol had an impact on crime, fear of crime and perception of the police. The results indicated that varying patrol strategies had no impact on any of the measured areas. The implications of this study are dramatic—randomly patrolling areas, rapid response and even doubling police presence had absolutely no impact on crime, fear of crime or what citizens thought about their police. Yet, random patrol and rapid response are still the most common patrol strategies used by law enforcement today! Forty years later, officers are still getting into their cruisers each day, driving around their patrol areas and waiting to be dispatched to calls.

While the KCPPE could certainly stand to be reproduced, the implications of the study are still important to consider. This experiment only further fueled theorists who had pushed for reform and change. Patrol strategies weren't working. There was an alarming divide between the people and the police. Police officers were no longer connected to the very communities that they served. Riots and protests were ongoing and a strong anti-police sentiment thrived. Something needed to change.

Community Policing Era (1980 – 2001?)

It was in this climate that police agencies entered into the Community Policing Era, officially beginning in 1980. In the early days of the community policing movement there were several notable cities that are considered to be the forerunners of putting this theory into practice. Cities such as Flint, Michigan, Newark, New Jersey and Newport News, Virginia are well known for their pioneering studies. Other important events during the early days of the era include James Q. Wilson and George Kelling's "Broken Windows" article in 1982 *(Wilson, 1982)*. The authors used a single broken window as a metaphor to illustrate how small incivilities and disorder in a neighborhood can create the potential for further crime. The overall conclusion was that disorder sets the stage for crime because it breeds fear of victimization, lessens pride and disintegrates community ties. These results could be extended to community policing theory by emphasizing a new focus on quality of life issues and community structure. In short, building strong community ties and paying attention to what might have been considered "the small stuff" could reduce crime, improve the quality of life and build a positive image of the police.

It was also during this era that Herman Goldstein's influential problem solving model known by the acronym SARA was introduced *(Goldstein, 1990)*. The model involves a clear and structured process of problem solving: Scan, analyze, respond and assess. This simple, yet thorough technique was quickly adopted

7

into the world of policing and became a staple part of community police officer training.

As the movement gained momentum various titles were applied to these problem-solving strategies and included such names as community-oriented policing, neighborhood-oriented policing and many others. In the end, it was community policing that stuck.

In 1994, the federal government created the Community Oriented Policing Services (COPS) office and citizens were promised 100,000 new police officers on the street. This was a time when the economy was stable and police agencies were properly funded. Applications from police administrators who were seeking grant money for the development of community police units flooded federal offices. Officers were hired, community police officers and specialized units were established and departments incorporated the words community policing into almost everything that they did.

The middle of the 1990s represented a peak in the Community Policing Era. New relationships between the police and the people were formed. Specialized programs to strengthen community ties were implemented. These included DARE, School Resource Officers, Neighborhood Watch, Citizen Police Academies and many, many others. Community partnerships were established, trust was built and some communities managed to have some shared power between citizens and police. Then things changed.

A New Era

On September 11, 2001, American policing was thrust in a new direction. Within a few hours, terrorists filled the citizens of the United States with fear. This message of fear was bolstered by politicians who spoke of the "axis of evil" and popularized a color-coded threat level chart. There was fear of more terrorist attacks, fear of anthrax, fear of biological warfare and fear of weapons of mass destruction.

This national fear of terror trickled down to city and municipal police officers in a variety of ways. Police executives were faced with new questions:

1. *Are you prepared for an attack on our city's schools?*

2. *Are you prepared for an anthrax exposure?*

3. *Are you prepared for an attack using biological warfare?*

4. *Can you provide adequate safety for major events in your community?*

5. *Are your officers properly trained for these new threats?*

6. *Can your agency handle a critical incident similar to the attacks in New York City?*

7. *Are your dispatchers prepared for major incidents?*

8. *Can you effectively communicate with other agencies during multiple agency incidents?*

These questions posed daunting challenges for police managers. To be able to prepare an agency to deal with these new threats, a lot of money was needed.

After 9/11 the community policing grants dried up. Money was reallocated for expenses related to critical incident response, interoperability and communications, protective equipment, training and a variety of other things that were deemed to be related to homeland security.

It is clear from this brief overview of American police history that the pendulum continues to swing back and forth. At one extreme are police officers riding around in cruisers with their windows up. They are completely disconnected from the communities that they serve and have no emphasis on building community partnerships. They use random, reactive patrol and value arrest numbers and clearance rates. On the other extreme is the officer walking around the schools, walking the streets or engaging in any one of hundreds of community service programs that have officers side by side with citizens. They are completely connected to residents and actively work to build trust and empathy with citizens. They use directed, proactive patrol and emphasize problem solving and the big picture. Since the peak of the Community Policing Era, the pendulum has clearly begun to swing back. It should be the goal of police leaders to stop that pendulum from swinging back too far and to strive to find a middle ground.

A final note on the historical overview of the evolution of American policing is that with all that has changed, from new technologies, to new Eras, to new fears, the daily activities of most police officers in the United States is strikingly similar to what it was 10, 20 or even 50 years ago. Taking reports of crime, responding to car accidents, dealing with inebriated individuals and handling basic calls for service still comprise the bulk of calls handled by today's rank and file police officers. These activities will continue to represent the fundamentals of daily policing but it is important to be aware of and respond to a higher goal set on long term solutions and preventative strategies. Today's police supervisors are faced with an ever-expanding list of duties and it is the challenge of these supervisors to best navigate through this new territory with confidence, thoughtfulness and diligence.

End Notes

Radelet, L.A. (1980). The police and the community. New York: Macmillan.

Kelling, G., Pate, T., Dieckman, D. and Brown, C. The Kansas City Preventative Patrol Experiment: A summary report. Washington, D.C.: Police Foundation (1974).

Goldstein, H. (1990). Problem-Oriented Policing. New York: McGraw-Hill.

Wilson, J., and Kelling, G. *Broken Windows: The police and neighborhood safety.*" Atlantic Monthly 249 (3): 29 – 38.

Community policing is one of the most commonly misunderstood terms in the entire history of law enforcement. The term has been emblazoned onto vehicles, incorporated into mission statements and emphasized on department websites. Despite an overwhelming push to adopt this idea, few know what community policing actually is. Only a small number of departments can be classified as true community policing agencies.

While teaching a recent class of 40 police officers, I asked if their departments operated using the community policing philosophy. The majority raised their hands, indicating that they did. When asked what they based this on, officers replied that their agencies used bike patrol, foot patrol, had a DARE officer or named other tangible programs. When asked what community policing was, most officers' answers were related to improved public relations or specific outreach programs. This has been a common belief about community policing among officers and citizens alike. However, a true community policing purist classifies it as "a philosophy and not a program." While many departments may utilize community programs, not all agencies with such programs are community policing agencies.

One can envision early theorists banging their heads against the wall as chief after chief and officer after officer swear their allegiance to the community policing concept and claim that they practice it. The fact is, most police departments do not practice community policing at all.

Special Focus 2.1:
Traditional Policing versus Community Policing

Traditional Policing	Community Policing
Narrow mission- arrest and statistics	Broad mission—expanded duties
Reactive (symptom-oriented)	Preventative (cause-oriented)
Random patrol	Directed patrol
"Us versus them" attitude	Community collaboration
Centralized command structure with strong chief (top-down)	Decentralized command structure with mini-chiefs (bottom-up)
Emphasis on short-term solutions	Emphasis on long-term solutions
Quantity	Quality
Efficient	Effective
Incident-driven	Problem solving
Conservative and rigid	Innovative and flexible

Community Policing Defined

Before assessing whether or not a particular agency is or is not operating under the umbrella of community policing, it is important to understand the meaning of this term. Researchers, theorists and police administrators alike have faced the daunting challenge of defining community policing.

The following are three definitions that emphasize the important elements of this philosophy:

1. "Community policing is a philosophy of full service personalized policing, where the same officer patrols the same area on a permanent basis, from a decentralized place, working in a proactive partnership with citizens to identify and solve problems" *(Trojanowicz, Woods, Harpold, Reboussin, & Trojanowicz, 1994, p. 6)*.

2. "Community policing is a policy and a strategy aimed at achieving more effective and efficient crime control, reduced fear of crime, improved quality of life, improved police services and police legitimacy, through a proactive reliance on community resources that seeks to change crime causing conditions. This assumes a need for a great accountability of police, greater public share in decision making, and greater concern for civil rights and liberties" *(Friedman, 1992, p. 4)*.

3. "Community policing is a philosophy that promotes organizational strategies, which support the systematic use of partnerships and problem-solving techniques, to proactively address the immediate conditions that give rise to public safety issues such as crime, social disorder, and fear of crime" (http://www.cops.usdoj.gov).

There are dozens of definitions offered to best characterize community policing. The process of attempting to define it has been an ongoing struggle for police administrators who seek clarity in order to best determine whether or not organizational goals have been met.

Identifying the Stakeholders

Once the concept is defined, it must be established who is involved in the process of community policing.

No police department can transition to this new philosophy without the support of several major stakeholders:

- **Police department:** This involves a commitment and understanding at all levels of the agency.

- **Members of the community:** This can involve people who live or work in the community or have some other connection to the city or town.

- **Politicians:** Local political figures will be important allies for community support, financial assistance and program development.

- **Business owners and employees:** It is quite common for these figures to participate in local meetings that address quality of life issues and safety because they understand the link between these concerns and a profitable business.

- **Media:** The media has an incredible amount of power and reaches a large audience. Developing positive connections with members of media is essential to the success of any community policing strategy.

- **Extended resources:** They may be located outside of the geographic community, but the resources that they offer will be of great assistance to many community outreach programs. It is important for the police to align with groups like rape crisis hotlines, domestic violence houses, Alcoholics Anonymous or any variety of mental health agencies. This helps reach particular groups of people who are in need of services beyond what a single officer can provide.

Key Elements of Community Policing

The philosophy of community policing has been defined. The stakeholders have been identified. The question still remains: *What does community policing involve? (Special Focus 2.1)*

There are specific essential elements of true community policing:

- **A broadened police mission:** Community policing theory stems from the fact that citizens have ever-expanding expectations of their police. In years past, the expectations were based on arresting criminals and responding to basic police calls such as medical emergencies, car accidents and physical fights. The duties of a police officer in the new millennium exceed far beyond traditional policing. Officers today must handle quality of life issues, assist the mentally ill, write and speak effectively, teach, conduct forensic investigations, engage in problem solving, excel at computer and technical skills and perform a myriad of other diverse duties. The community policing philosophy recognizes these broad responsibilities and encourages a new way of thinking about the role that police should play in society.

- **Department-wide philosophy:** One of the cornerstones of true community policing is the necessity that the philosophy is understood and adopted by every member of a department. Administrators and executives must embrace it and need to communicate with the rank and file so that members understand the expanded mission and the long-term, preventative goals.

- **Decentralized command structure:** Community policing requires an entirely new management system that is inconsistent with the quasi-military, centralized and rigid structure of the Reform Era. It requires that the standard organizational chart with a chief on top be flipped upside down so that each patrol officer becomes a "mini chief." This type of structure allows officers more flexibility in decision-making and encourages discretion.

- **Shift from reactive to proactive strategies:** Traditional police practices emphasize reactive policing—officers drive around and wait to be dispatched to incidents. Officers arrive, quickly deal with the situation and clear the scene as soon as possible to make themselves available for the next call. Community policing directs officers to identify the root cause of problems so that issues can be addressed. Early intervention is the key to prevention. Value is placed on prevented crimes instead of arrest statistics or, quality versus quantity.

- **Problem solving:** In an effort to work proactively to prevent crime officers and community members are encouraged to collaborate in order to identify underlying issues so that problems and quality of life issues can be creatively resolved. The goal is to prevent police officers from being a quick fix or band-aid answer and to instead focus on long-term solutions. The old push to get in and out fast has been abandoned so that officers do not continually respond to the same locations, again and again, for the same issues. Quality of life issues are heavily emphasized.

- **Collaboration and partnerships:** Community policing emphasizes a team approach to problem solving. The team involves not only police but the various members of the communities that they serve. Working with residents and business owners is essential to effectively solve problems. It also narrows the division between the people and their police and empowers community members. The concerns of the public are the concerns of the police.

- **Community building/structure:** The Broken Windows theory identified the need to build structure and pride in a community *(Wilson, 1982)*. Disorder breeds chaos and crime. With this knowledge in mind community policing units were originally designed to go out into communities to build structure through meetings, open communication and problem solving. Once these neighborhood groups were successful, the officers could transition from leaders to resources and allow those communities to flourish on their own with the community police officers playing a diminished role.

- **Accountability:** A final component of community policing is accountability. Every member of an agency must be held accountable for their individual actions. This is a change from earlier police hierarchies that encouraged the flow of responsibility up the chain of command. Under the community policing model, with an emphasis on decentralized management and increases in discretion and responsibility, the rank and file accept more accountability for their actions. One way to accomplish this is to assign officers to the same beat areas every day. Consistency in beat assignments gives officers a sense of ownership over "their" areas and also provides a recognizable face to those community members who live and work within those areas. This concept involves all patrol officers working in consistent areas and also involves the assignment of other officers to work in designated areas as Community Policing Officers (CPOs).

Early researchers recognized the inherent challenges for a police department moving from traditional policing strategies to the new philosophy of community policing. The true integration requires dramatic changes in management styles, the rigid and well-established command structure, citizen relationships, and a complete overhaul of standard operating procedures. At the onset of the Community Policing Era, theorists estimated that it would take an average agency about 10 – 15 years to fully integrate all of the essential elements of community policing into their everyday practices. As time went on however, the question of how long it would take agencies to transition became less relevant. New questions arose challenging whether police agencies could make the transition at all.

End Notes

Friedman, R. R. (1992). *Community policing: Comparative perspectives and prospects.* New York: St. Martin's Press.

Trojanowicz, R. D., Woods, D., Harpold, J., Reboussin, R. & Trojanowicz, S. (1994). *Community policing: A survey of police departments in the United States.* Washington, DC: Government Printing Office.

U.S. Department of Justice (DOJ). *Office of community oriented policing services.* Retrieved September 15, 2009, from http://www.cops.usdoj.gov.

Wilson, J. Q., & Kelling, G. L. (1982, March). Broken windows: The police and neighborhood safety. *Atlantic Monthly, 256,* 29 – 38.

The term "community policing" spread like wildfire throughout the law enforcement community. Police administrators, citizens and researchers latched onto the popular term that inspired community partnerships, problem solving and an expanding role for police. Early support for this idea came from every angle and it was as if community policing could do no wrong. Community policing teams, specialized patrol assignments, bike units, outreach programs and almost any piece of equipment that could be associated with community policing received financial support from residents, businesses and government agencies at all levels. The concept boomed in the mid- to late-1980s and peaked again in the mid-1990s as a result of President Clinton's promise of 100,000 new police officers on the streets.

Identifying the Problems with Community Policing

From the beginning, with the majority of police departments scrambling to get on board with this popular policing concept, there have been staunch critics. They range from police executives and the rank and file, to criminal justice researchers and community members. Over the years a laundry list of major problems has been developed that identifies exactly why community policing cannot be successfully implemented in the current culture of American policing.

With the increasing recognition that so many agencies have not been able to fully transition to this new philosophy, it is important to consider the essential elements that contribute to this decades-long struggle.

- **Lack of tangible definition/understanding of concept:**
  The original theorists have identified poor implementation as one of the major reasons that community policing has not survived in so many departments. In many cases

administrators grabbed onto the buzzword more than the philosophy and attempted to transition without fully understanding what the term meant. Even to this day many police officers do not have a solid understanding of community policing and continue to liken it to programs and patrol strategies instead of a change in philosophy, management and overall departmental goals.

- **Quasi-military hierarchy/bureaucracy is inconsistent with community policing:** One of the essential elements of an effective community policing organization is a decentralized, creative, discretionary approach with mini-chiefs for each geographic area. No agency can effectively adopt community policing without dramatically changing long-practiced management styles that emphasize powerful managers and adherence to a rigid command structure. In 1989 Lee Brown stated, "The military model is totally inappropriate for community policing" *(Brown, 1989).* Those upper ranking administrators who worked throughout their careers to make it to the top have been reluctant to shake the familiar hierarchy by relinquishing power and control to the rank and file.

- **Natural resistance to change:** Part of the initial implementation problem was that the transition to being a community policing agency was forced on many of the street-level personnel. Administrators who had researched the philosophy, attended training sessions on it and who understood its value failed to take the time to explain the concept to other agency members. Instead, they just started making changes with little or no warning. People naturally resist change and new concepts that are not explained and not understood will rarely be warmly received. Those administrators who did try to get everyone on board faced resistance from officers who believed that it threatened the status quo, would be more work and was outside of their regular duties.

- **Lack of veteran officers and candidates who have the required characteristics to engage in community policing:** The job of policing has certainly expanded. With the many hats that today's officers are wearing, the typical officer must be able to interrogate sex offenders, fight with suspects, testify in court, use computers and other pieces of technology, pursue fleeing vehicles, write detailed and articulate reports, interact positively with the public, participate in community outreach programs, handle and process forensic evidence, be sensitive to special victims, be thorough, be professional, be fit, be able to multi-task, have integrity and the list goes on. Who is this superhero? While this may be the ideal candidate and the best fit for a community policing agency, these people are few and far between. Administrators are forced to work with what they have and must make hiring decisions from diminishing applicant pools. This model officer is a rarity and not all officers are suited for these diverse duties.

- **Abuse of Community Police Officer (CPO) assignments:** One of the essential cornerstones of community policing is beat consistency. This can be accomplished by assigning patrol officers to the same areas each day and/or by assigning specific officers to work as CPOs who are then assigned to high-need areas. In many cases, CPOs do not respond to general calls for service and are instead tasked with strengthening community partnerships and problem solving. These duties require working flexible hours and adjusting schedules and days off. As a result of these highly desirable and flexible schedules, compared with traditional regimented shift work, some officers request CPO assignments for the perceived perks and not because of their commitment to the overall community philosophy. A 1993 study revealed that officers in New York City were asked why they became CPOs and the number one answer was flexible hours (68%). The second reason given was for the fixed days off (56%). Only 34% said it was to increase community involvement *(McElroy, 1993)*.

21

- **Division between CPOs and "regular patrol officers":** As specialized units began to actualize within police agencies, it didn't take long for a rift to develop between the CPOs and the rest of the patrol force. CPOs have more flexible schedules and often do not have to respond to regular calls for service. They are somewhat removed from traditional patrol duties and these differences can breed resentment. An unanticipated outcome occurred when the rank and file fostered bitterness for the entire community policing philosophy because they resented CPOs. A line was drawn in the sand between community police officers and traditional patrol officers. Inattentive supervisors who failed to remedy this problem early on, only further contributed to this issue.

  A further issue occurred when community policing units dissolved and CPOs were re-assigned back to patrol, retired, resigned or were given different duties. It left the very patrol officers who had developed a long-standing dislike for community policing to fill the gaps left by the CPOs. To further complicate this issue, despite the loss of these specialized units, citizens had broadened their expectations of their police departments and many patrol officers were unprepared and resistant.

- **Money/funding:** Policing is not a for-profit business and funding has little to do with success or failure. If programs are wildly successful and well liked, it does not protect them from being cut when budgets get tight. The recent economy has certainly proven that as departments continue to face an onslaught of fiscal cuts, they are forced to select what stays and what goes. Unfortunately for community policing, it is often these positions that tend to get cut first as they are sometimes viewed as less critical than traditional patrol officers.

- **New Era with a new focus:** During the 1970s, when friction was palpable between the people and their police, images and stories of poor police conduct, corruption and excessive force dominated the media and invoked anger in the minds of many Americans. Fairness, equality, justice, accountability, community involvement, empathy, respect and integrity were demanded. These values remained prominent throughout the first few decades of the Community Policing Era. After 9/11, new issues arose. Fear, terrorism, school safety, biohazards, chemical warfare and national security stepped into the spotlight. These fresh concerns redirected national, state and local financial resources to new training, technology and policy development, all oriented toward preparing for these new threats.

Despite the fact that today's police agencies existed decades into the Community Policing Era, the majority failed to fully adopt this philosophy. All of the aforementioned factors have contributed to this and it is for these reasons that full metamorphosis has not and will not work for the majority of police departments in America *(Special Focus 3.1)*. However, even with this massive failure to fully transition, community relationships have dramatically improved from where they were at the onset of this new era. A comparative analysis of public-police relations then and now would reveal impressive positive improvements.

It is difficult to point to one specific change that is responsible for this dramatic shift in police-community relations. Some may cite specific programs, changes in policies, media attention, increased accountability or to the general societal adaptations that have occurred over the past few decades. In truth, the change has been fueled by many factors, some within police agencies and some external to them. Either way, it would be naïve to believe that the community policing philosophy did not significantly aid in this dramatic improvement in relations. It is for this reason that many of the basic tenets of community policing should be valued and recognized as the catalyst for cultivating better bonds between police and civilians.

Police executives and officers who may have experienced frustration and hopelessness at a department's failed attempt to become true community police agencies should stay hopeful. The pressure is off. The era is over. While community policing cleared the path for stronger citizen partnerships and proactive policing, we have entered into a new age of professionalism, community relationships, technology and a new insight into how to effectively respond to crime and quality of life issues. Today's police supervisors should recognize the value of proactive and preventative police strategies. Further, they should keep in mind what police-community relationships were like in the 1970s and how many positive strides have been made over the past few decades. With that knowledge in mind it is time to move forward into this new Era and to re-evaluate the needs of the department and the needs of the community.

Special Focus 3.1: the Challenges of Implementing Community Policing at the Northampton, Massachusetts Police Department

In 1994 the Department of Justice (DOJ) heavily promoted the community policing concept. Grant funding and specialized training was available to those departments that committed to work toward making the transition to this popular philosophy. The Northampton, Massachusetts Police Department had a newly appointed chief, Russell P. Sienkiewicz, who supported this popular and progressive philosophy. The chief's plan included the formation of a new Community Services Unit (CSU). The members of this section would work proactively, in collaboration with citizens, to identify problems and work toward solutions.

Sergeant Brian Rust had already been working as a DARE officer and as a crime prevention officer. He was familiar with community policing strategies and had established lines of open communication with various community groups and individuals. He was charged with managing the new unit. To staff the community services unit, existing personnel were asked to submit letters of interest and individuals were interviewed by a panel, consisting of both police representatives and community stockholders, and selected to fill the following positions:

- 1 School Resource Officer for the high school
- 1 School Resource Officer for the middle school
- 3 Community Resource Officers who were assigned to targeted areas of the city

The unit also included one DARE Officer, who had already been working in that capacity.

The five new positions were funded using a Department of Justice, Universal Hiring Program grant. The grant required that the officers work in the area of community policing and that the employer make every effort to retain the employees once the grant term of three years had expired. There was subsequent extension of this funding under the COPS program.

Recognizing the challenges associated with such a significant change, police administrators made significant efforts to make the transition easier for staff.

- Trainers from the DOJ reviewed the department and made recommendations to ease the transition. They also conducted extensive training for the personnel who were assigned to the Community Policing Unit.

- Additional training was conducted by Dr. David Carter, a nationally known authority on community policing for department members.

- The chief addressed all personnel and explained the role of the CSU and the expectations of line officers and supervisors regarding the department's community policing efforts.

- Sgt. Rust created training material and met with all supervisors to explain the CSU and how the CSU would function as part of the department as a whole.

- A city-wide survey was conducted to measure citizen satisfaction with police services and their concerns and perceptions about crime and quality of life issues.

The community services unit was initially successful. In recognition of the importance of community policing, Sgt. Rust was promoted to lieutenant and the section was elevated from a unit to the Community Services Bureau (CSB). The bureau was located in an office space in a separate building, due to lack of adequate space in the existing police facility. Even with the CSB's successes, it didn't take long for significant resistance to create distance between the CSB and other police personnel. Captain Joseph Koncas identified some of the challenges faced by CSB personnel as:

- Making the transition from reactive to proactive policing.

- Becoming self-disciplined to work in a less-structured environment (working independently with minimal supervision).

- Becoming problem solvers and thinking outside the box.

- Being held to higher expectations for performance and personal carriage.

- Maintaining peer (patrol) acceptance/approval.

- Being located off-site due to lack of office space at the police station.

When asked how the patrol force responded to this new idea, Captain Koncas went on to address some issues specific to patrol/CSB friction. As the community policing section was implemented and began functioning many within the department viewed the concept with skepticism and were reluctant to embrace this new idea. Some patrol officers may have felt that the transition to this new form of policing somehow implied that what they had been doing was not working. They may have felt less important and valued as employees and public servants. Additionally, CSB personnel had certain perks that other patrol officers may have been envious of. These benefits included flexible hours, minimal supervision, more training opportunities, private and separate work spaces, take home vehicles and access to the newest technology. Finally, CSB officers had positive contact with the public that sometimes generated media attention and public accolades.

Interestingly, traditional patrol officers did benefit from CSB activities. If CSB officers were on duty, calls for service in targeted areas would be handled by the associated resource officer. Additionally, calls that required follow-up investigation or that involved individuals living in certain areas could also be re-assigned from the initial patrol officer to the CSB officer assigned to that area of the City. Issues inside schools were given to School Resource and DARE officers. CSB members were also fantastic resources if officers or detectives were in need of specific information regarding students, residents or even visitors. Community Service personnel were extremely familiar with social networks and personal relationships and this information could prove invaluable to investigators. Finally, the CSB did improve the public's image of the police. People on the street were friendlier toward the police and were more likely to talk with them and provide them with information.

Despite these overwhelming advantages, the divide between traditional patrol officers and the CSB continued to grow. This was felt by CSB members who felt dejected by their former friends who no longer viewed them as "real police officers." Over time, the Bureau began to crumble. One by one, members of the community services section left. Some didn't just leave the CSB, they left the department, well before their retirement dates. Citing a variety of personal reasons, every single member of the CSB, with the exception of the original DARE officer and one community resource officer who returned to patrol, resigned from the department.

Regarding the failure of the department to retain these valuable personnel, Captain Koncas indicated that burnout was probably the main reason. Problem-solving is draining and these officers had been placed in new positions where there was a lot of work to be done. Secondly, the prospect of returning to the more rigid and structured work environment within traditional patrol may not have been appealing to these individuals who had grown accustomed to greater flexibility and less supervision. Finally, CSB members worked on identified problems and were able to collaborate with citizens to implement change. Koncas believes that returning to the more reactive form of incident-driven patrol would not have been as rewarding and the daily activities may have been too mundane.

As this attrition was occurring, police administrators encouraged patrol personnel to submit letters of interest in these now vacant positions. There was little, if any interest, and, as of 2009, the department appears as it did before 1994. There is no CSB and one DARE officer.

Regarding the lack of interest in the CSB vacancies, Captain Koncas noted that CSB positions were "not for officers who just wanted to get by." These assignments required significant effort in the form of self-management and self-initiated activity. Additionally, the patrol force had developed a dismissive attitude toward the efforts of the CSB as a whole, that existing members may have been hesitant to join.

Although the budget is putting significant pressure on community policing efforts and, in some departments, has resulted in the total loss of these sections, Captain Koncas hopes that one day the Northampton Police Department will see a return to this form of policing. Despite the fact that the CSB has since dissolved, there were many successes within this program. The captain does acknowledge that if any of the original CSB positions are filled again they would not operate within a separate CSB. Instead, they would remain well entrenched in the patrol section.

Is this an example of success or failure? In truth, it is probably a little bit of both. Despite significant administrative efforts to implement this change, the rank and file never fully accepted the community policing philosophy. The CSB members were not seen as real police officers and were instead viewed as privileged employees who received the public's praise without doing the dirty work. Over time, the emphasis and interest in community policing waned. On the flip side, the CSB officers did very well applying the basic principles of community policing to the issues faced by citizens within their assigned areas. The public's image of the police improved as the department generated positive media attention and individual communications. The question then becomes not so much whether or not community policing was a failure, because it was not. It was the implementation and acceptance of community policing that failed.

Reprinted with permission from Captain Joseph Koncas, Northampton Police Dept.

End Notes

Brown, L. P. (1989, September). "Community policing: A practical guide for police officials," Perspectives on Policing, No. 12. Washington, DC: U.S. Department of Justice, National Institute of Justice; and Harvard University.

McElroy, J. E., Cosgrove, C. A., & Sadd, S. (1993). Community policing: The CPOP in New York. Newbury Park, CA: Sage Publications.

Carter, D. L. (2002). *The police and the community* (7th ed.). Upper Saddle River, NJ: Pearson Education, Inc.

Goldstein, H. (1990). *Problem-oriented policing.* New York: McGraw-Hill, Inc.

Kelling, G. L., Pate, A. M., Dieckman, D., & Brown, C. (1974). *The Kansas City preventative patrol experiment: Technical report.* Washington, DC: Police Foundation.

Radelet, L. A., & Reed, H. C. (1980). *The police and the community* (3rd ed.). New York: MacMillan.

Wilson, J. Q., & Kelling, G. L. (1982, March). Broken windows: The police and neighborhood safety. *Atlantic Monthly,* 256, 29 – 38.

The 1980s represented the peak of the Community Policing Era as the concepts of proactive problem solving and community collaboration generated instantaneous support. The decade also marked the onset of an aggressive anti-drug campaign at all levels of government and almost universal support for anything related to drug prevention and enforcement. The mid-1990s experienced a second peak, with Bill Clinton's promise of 100,000 new police officers on the street, an infusion that was designed to augment existing Community Policing Units and associated activities. During these decades, community policing initiatives and concepts received a lot of attention from community members, government agencies, politicians and businesses, and, consequently, a lot of financial support.

The events of 9/11 shifted the focus away from local community issues and instead toward fear, terrorism and domestic preparedness for major incidents. With the nation's eyes staring down a global threat, money that was once allocated for community policing activities was rerouted to a new catch phrase: Homeland security.

Under the umbrella of homeland security in the new century, law enforcement has narrowed its focus to issues that had received little attention prior to the terrorist attacks in 2001. The new emphasis is on terrorism, school safety, response to mass casualty incidents, biological warfare and threats to information and computer security. Although many police agencies had policies and procedures in place to handle these issues and many officers had attended some training, it was nowhere near the level of preparedness that was required to best respond to these potentially emergent threats.

With the new focus on homeland security and new threats and challenges facing today's officers and administrators, it is important to take a moment to address and discuss specific factors that have changed over the past decade and that greatly affect the way police agencies are managed and led.

31

Terrorism

Although many researchers and practitioners in the field of law enforcement in 2000 may have wondered if the Community Policing Era had come to an end after countless agencies struggled and failed to make the transition, it was the events of 9/11 that definitively answered that question. The day that terrorists attacked and killed thousands of people on American soil was the day that law enforcement agencies shifted gears. Suddenly police administrators were evaluating their policies and procedures for critical incidents and writing new ones. They were assessing their supplies and buying gas masks and Tyvec suits. They were looking over their training curriculum and redeveloping it. They were looking at their cities and identifying possible terrorist targets. They were rerouting officers from traditional training to Incident Command training involving mass casualties and multi-agency response.

Terrorism and the possibility of further attacks is now an everyday consideration. There has been an increase in contact with federal agencies as the FBI and the Department of Homeland Security work to share information about potential threats. Terrorism, though seemingly far away from Anytown, USA, has become a familiar and daunting possibility for police administrators nationwide.

Interoperability

Along with the new focus on terrorist threats, police managers have been forced to evaluate their agency's ability to communicate with other agencies during a critical incident. One of the problems identified in the aftermath of 9/11 was the difficulties that first responders had communicating with each other while at the scene and responding to the World Trade Centers. This issue highlighted the limitations that many agencies have regarding inter-agency communication. As a result, police managers have been working diligently with other departments to build and maintain improved radio systems that allow for better inter-agency communications on scenes that have a multi-agency response.

Funding

The majority of police departments today are facing dramatic financial cutbacks. A lot of federal and state funding is restricted to those agencies who demonstrate that the money will be used for anti-terrorism efforts and homeland security. Training curriculums have changed. Technological needs have changed. It is easier to get funding for critical incident training, communications systems, specialized equipment, or high-level computer software, than it is to get funding for School Resource Officers or DARE Officers.

Due to this fiscal transition many community policing units and/or positions are disappearing as these officers are being absorbed back into the patrol force. This trend is illustrated by a series of Bureau of Justice Statistics surveys on the total number of full-time community police officers: 1997 = 15,978, 1999 = 91,072 *(DOJ, 2001, p. 2, Table 2)*, 2000 = 102,598 *(DOJ, 2003, p. 15, Table 32)* and in 2003 that number dropped to 54,849 *(DOJ, 2006, p. 20, Table 42)*.

Community Expectations

Despite shrinking budgets and the resulting reduction of personnel, community members still expect strong connections with their police departments, accountability, professionalism, programming, integrity and openness. This has caused the onus of outreach activities to fall on the shoulders of the street-level patrol force. Administrators also feel a pressure to maintain and lead a department that meets these demands.

Technology

Changes in technology seem to be moving forward at an alarming rate. Computers that are cutting edge one year are out of date two years later. That same problem arises with various forms of technology including cell phones, PDA's, digital cameras and a wide variety of other items. This is difficult for police department administrators because they rely on extremely limited annual budgets and constantly updating equipment is difficult and sometimes impossible.

Technology reaches far beyond commonly known devices like cameras and computers. There have been significant developments in the area of less than lethal force options. Items include rubber bullets, tasers, pepper ball guns and other creative weapons that aim to stop suspects in their tracks. Citizens may not want to fund these purchases, but may be quick to criticize an agency when an officer is involved in a use of force situation and does not make use of alternative force methods.

There have also been developments in crime scene service tools that involve evidence recording and collection. Once again, citizens who routinely watch popular television shows may expect their police agencies to have access to this high-tech equipment.

There are a wide variety of other options in the area of technology. In-cruiser cameras, stop sticks, license plate scanners, traffic violation cameras, surveillance systems, computer software … the list goes on and on. The current generation of employees and citizens expect that police departments make use of cutting edge technology. It doesn't take long for a department to fall behind in the world of "the latest and greatest." While effective and efficient technology is incredibly important to the Millennial, that standard is usually applied to the essentials—such as computers, phones and cameras. Other pieces of advanced equipment are a perk, but not a necessity to make citizens and employees content. Progressive police administrators should strive to keep their essential equipment up to date and fully operational. Additionally, they should seek out new technologies that will best meet the needs of their individual agency.

Media

In the last 20 years the global media has also experienced dramatic changes. There are more forms of media and information centers than ever before. The typical newspaper, magazine and television outlets have now expanded to include online news sources, blogs, texts, digital video, YouTube, social networking sites and many more. A police use of force incident that happens on Main Street in Philadelphia can be watched on digital video on a cell phone in under a minute on the other side of the globe. Never has there been a time when information travels so quickly.

As has always been the case, the media has a significant impact on people's perceptions. People often believe what they see in the media. It is for this reason that police administrators must work tirelessly to maintain strong contacts with members of the press and to provide positive media information whenever possible.

Professionalism/Accountability

Never has there been a time when police officers are held to the standards that they are held to today. Officers are constantly monitored by their peers, supervisors, other police agencies and by community members as a whole. If they engage in any behavior that is borderline questionable, they stand to be investigated and disciplined. Officers are criticized for their appearance, how they drive, how they talk with people, how fast or slow they respond to an incident, how they use force and how they spend their meal break. Officers lead very public lives and are highly visible for public scrutiny. Because of this, officers are held to extremely high standards. Interview committees seek candidates with impeccable backgrounds and personal character. Present day police departments face the challenge of successfully recruiting and retaining these unique candidates.

Education

Hand in hand with professionalism is the increased attention to the value of a college education. More and more departments are seeking candidates with a college degree. To be competitive, many police candidates are attending college, studying criminal justice and are applying for jobs with a four-year college degree in hand. Along with this change in the typical police candidate, some departments have modified their promotional standards to include minimum qualifications that include a Bachelor's or Master's degree.

In addition to formal college educations, departments have also increased the number of training hours that officers are required to attend each year. Academies have expanded their training material as well as the way in which it is presented with in-service and online curriculum. The overall trend in this area is an increase in education and training for all officers and supervisors.

It is clear that the nation is in a new era. The focus of policing has been modified to include emergent threats and fresh challenges. However, even with these expanding duties and financial cutbacks, community members still maintain high expectations of their police officers and want their needs met. They expect openness, accountability and professionalism. They expect officers to be educated, possess the most advanced technology and be aware of contemporary issues in the field. The progressive police leader of this century understands the changes in these areas and is able to use that knowledge to successfully supervise and lead his police department into the complex and ever-changing future.

End Notes

U.S. Department of Justice (DOJ), Bureau of Justice Statistics. (2001, February). *Community policing in local police departments, 1997 and 1999.* NCJ 184794. Washington, DC: U.S. Government Printing Office.

U.S. Department of Justice (DOJ), Bureau of Justice Statistics. (2003, January). *Local police departments, 2000.* NCJ 196002. Washington, DC: U.S. Government Printing Office.

U.S. Department of Justice, Bureau of Justice Statistics. (2006, May). *Local police departments, 2003.* NCJ 210118. Washington, DC: U.S. Government Printing Office.

I t is the constant challenge of every police chief to keep up with changes in technology, training, equipment and patrol strategies so that the needs of the community can best be met. In this new era with a focus on terrorism and homeland security, it is the right time for re-evaluation. Assessing past objectives and defining future goals is essential, as the national climate of the 1980s varies greatly from today. While the general concept of "to protect and serve" still holds true, how that is accomplished is ever-changing. Under this rather ambiguous term, more specific goals need to be defined.

Mission Statements

Many agencies that worked toward implementing a community policing philosophy began by modifying existing mission statements or by establishing mission statements where one had never been written. Mission statements often include some goals of an agency, such as to reduce crime and to provide a high quality of life for the citizens that are served (Special Focus 5.1). While mission statements are a useful technique to highlight general objectives of an agency, a more complete list of goals will be a constructive compliment to existing statements.

Special Focus 5.1: Sample Mission Statements

These seven mission statements were collected randomly from the websites of police departments across the United States. While they vary in length, each has a similar focus. Words such as partnership, community, integrity and the term quality of life are reoccurring themes. Mission statements are a good starting point to establish a progressive and unified department.

37

"It is the Mission of the Wichita Falls Police Department to help preserve a better quality of life through a partnership with the citizens based on unbiased law enforcement and a desire to serve."

–Wichita Falls, Texas Police Department
http://www.cwftx.net/index.aspx?nid=133

"The Mission of the New York City Police Department is to enhance the quality of life in our City by working in partnership with the community and in accordance with constitutional rights to enforce the laws, preserve the peace, reduce fear, and provide for a safe environment."

– New York City, New York Police Department
http://www.nyc.gov/html/nypd/html/home/mission.shtml

"The Chicago Police Department, as part of, and empowered by the community, is committed to protect the lives, property and rights of all people, to maintain order and to enforce the law impartially. We will provide quality police service in partnership with other members of the community. To fulfill our mission, we will strive to attain the highest degree of ethical behavior and professional conduct at all times."

– Chicago, Illinois Police Department
https://portal.chicagopolice.org/portal/page/portal/ClearPath/
News/Statistical%20Reports/Annual%20Reports/1998%20Annual%20
Reports/98Introduction.pdf

"It is the mission of the Albany Police Department to serve all people with integrity and respect, while enhancing the quality of their lives. The department is committed to the service of the community through efficient and effective policing, maintaining the highest level of integrity, ethics and honesty while promoting the professionalism of departmental personnel and treating the public with respect and dignity regardless of an individual's demographic background."

– Albany, New York Police Department
http://www.albanyny.org/Government/Departments/Police.aspx

"The mission of the Atlanta Police Department is to reduce crime and promote the quality of life, in partnership with our community."
– Atlanta, Georgia Police Department
http://www.atlantapd.org/

"Our mission, together with the communities of Miami, is to make our city a place where all people can live, work, and visit safely without fear."
– Miami, Florida Police Department
http://www.miami-police.org/about.html

Identifying Specific Goals

The purpose of establishing specific goals is so that they can each be individually assessed to determine how the department can work toward them. Tangible strategies can be identified and put into action. With that in mind, ***the following list contains the probable goals of most police agencies,*** although every department is different and would want to create its own list, specific to the unique needs of that community.

- **Reduce crime and reduce fear of crime:** Perhaps the most obvious goal of all police agencies is the prevention/reduction of crime and the associated reduction of fear of criminal activity. Law enforcement's historical roots are founded in crime suppression and prevention. Over time, however, the job of a police officer has greatly expanded to include many more diverse duties.

- **Contribute to a high quality of life in the community:** Quality of life issues are a key component in effective policing, and for good reason. People's perceptions of the police and of their community, as a whole, often come down to seemingly simple quality of life issues. Concerns of loud music/partying, litter, graffiti, barking dogs or unsightly properties, should be addressed. Left unattended, these issues can balloon into more serious incidents of personal violence or substantial property damage.

39

They can lead to friction and frustration. Tending to smaller issues may also contribute to community pride and a reduced fear of crime.

- **Positive community contact:** Positive relationships with community members and visitors are critical components of successful policing. As was indicated earlier in this book, strong community ties create a symbiotic relationship between the people and their police.

- **Community involvement:** Related to the previous goal, community involvement is an essential building block in establishing positive contacts. Additionally, having citizens working with police officers and participating in police-related programs, will likely result in an enhanced understanding of the challenges of police work. An involved community is one that is more likely to support its department.

- **Active focus on communication:** At the root of so many issues internal and external to a department is communication; poor communication, no communication or miscommunication leads to frustration on behalf of all involved parties. Employees may feel they are treated unfairly or citizens may feel that their police department is hiding information. These types of issues lead to mistrust, frustration and anger both internally and externally. It is for this reason that communication needs to be specifically listed as a goal so that administrators can actively work toward openness. Information should flow freely up and down the ranks and back and forth with community members.

- **Preparedness for new threats:** It has always been the goal of police officers to prepare for the variety of incidents that they may face in their daily duties. However, the recent change in national focus from smaller threats to global terrorism and other critical incidents has forced administrators and trainers to better prepare police forces for these new threats. Incidents such as school shootings and biochemical exposures have forced all emergency personnel to re-evaluate their training, equipment and readiness for mass casualties and critical incidents.

- **Positive public image:** It has been past practice for many police executives to sit back and let their public image be created for them. This image is based on many elements including individual interactions with members of an agency, media coverage, police/community activities, accreditation status, integrity, crime data and departmental presentation such as uniform, station, vehicles, pamphlets, recruiting posters and websites. Administrators need to accept that while there is a portion of their image that they cannot control, there is a sizeable piece that they can control. Businesses in the private sector understand this well and in response have marketing strategies that aim to improve their image. While active marketing may seem unfamiliar to police administrators and perhaps out of place in the public sector, its use is invaluable.

- **Public understanding of police function/operation:** One of the many consequences of police work being so heavily portrayed on television and in movies is that the public has a skewed perspective regarding the role and abilities of police officers. Common misconceptions include the number of police officers on the street (citizens are likely to think it is much higher than it is), the amount of time it takes officers to complete a criminal investigation (they believe incidents will be resolved quickly) and the ability of officers to locate and successfully process evidence (many believe that forensic evidence is present at every scene and that officers can quickly collect and process it to reveal the identity of the suspect). These misguided beliefs also affect candidates interested in law enforcement as a career, who believe that the daily activities of a typical officer are comprised of car chases and shootings instead of interviews and report writing. The most successful way to combat misconceptions about police activity is to provide outreach and education programs for community members.

- **Recruitment:** It is no secret that interest in police work has declined substantially over the past few decades. Despite a slight patriotic surge in interest after 9/11, there has been a steady reduction in applications. According to Jennifer Boyter, a spokeswoman for the International Association of Chiefs of Police, "The shortage of new officers is one of the top concerns facing law enforcement across the country" *(Hench, 2006)*. Where one vacancy used to attract 100 people, now a department may be lucky to have 40 or 50 interested candidates. Once candidates have taken the written exam, psychological assessment, physical fitness test, and have passed a criminal background check, that number quickly dwindles down to perhaps 7 – 10 qualified applicants. Finally, with the expanding duties of today's police officers and the importance of strong personal characteristics, communication skills and intelligence, the interview panel may find it difficult to identify the right candidate out of the remaining pool. It is for this reason that police administrators should be actively engaging in recruitment methods that reach a wide variety of individuals. They should seek potential candidates who excel at interpersonal/written communication, who enjoy problem solving and who feel comfortable with new technology. These people may not have considered a career in law enforcement or be enrolled in a criminal justice program. By seeking these less traditional candidates, administrators will further broaden their existing workforce. Department leaders who are seeking diverse candidates will need to identify specific strategies that will reach these minority populations *(Special Focus 5.2)*. Much like actively marketing to improve a public image, proactively recruiting candidates may also be a fairly new concept to police executives who used to sit back while people fought for positions. It is the new challenge of administrators to create successful strategies in this area.

- **Create/maintain a positive working environment:** While this concept would likely be omitted from the majority of lists identifying departmental goals, it is as critical as all of the others. Healthy working environments emphasize open communication, freedom for creativity, room for new challenges and opportunities, respect, fairness and equality. This positive working atmosphere will improve morale and retention. In turn, this will improve the interactions that officers have on the streets every day, thereby contributing to a positive public image and strong community relationships.

Special Focus 5.2: Recruiting Strategies

Proactive recruitment is a necessity to develop a diverse workforce. There are a number of specific steps that can be taken in order to attract a more diverse pool of applicants.

Create and Maintain a Diverse Recruitment Team: Recruitment staff should reflect the type of candidates that the agency is trying to attract. Interested candidates are more likely to approach recruiters who are most similar to themselves.

Create and Maintain a Department Website Aimed at Recruiting: The majority of people interested in working for a specific department will visit that agency's website to learn as much as possible about their potential employer. In addition to have a professional website that is informative and user-friendly, the site developers should also keep recruitment in mind. Pictures of officers on the job and working in a variety of positions are an effective recruitment tool. Like the recruitment team, officers pictured should be reflective of those individuals that an agency is trying to attract.

Recruit from Non-traditional Locations: Traditional recruiters can be found setting up tables at career fairs held at colleges with criminal justice programs. That has been the standard in recruiting efforts for decades. However, there are many potential candidates outside of this realm who have simply never considered being a police officer and who would be responsive to informative recruiters who can discuss the benefits and opportunities associated with a career in policing. Recruiters should attend career fairs at colleges without criminal justice programs, but instead with a large liberal arts focus. Additionally, recruiters would benefit from putting up posters in gyms, sports arenas, military bases and other facilities that emphasize fitness and excitement.

Create and Maintain Diverse Mentors: When potential applicants assess an agency, they may check to see of minority candidates have been able to move into specialized units and have attained positions of rank. If it appears that minority officers are not given equal opportunities, interested candidates may be less likely to apply. This does not mean that specific candidates with minority status should be promoted above others. Instead, administrators should be cognizant of this issue and should seek to establish equality and fairness in the workplace.

Create and Maintain Positive Community Contacts: Many officers who are on the job today submitted their initial applications because they had a friend who was a police officer or heard about upcoming entrance exams through friendly interactions with police personnel. Face to face contacts and their potential to positively impact applicant pools should not be overlooked. Recruitment is a department-wide task and this should be conveyed to all personnel.

Source: Kasper, J. (2006, December). Proven Steps for Recruiting Women. *Law and Order*, 54 (12), 63 – 67.

Articulating these goals is an effective way to provide clarity for departments that were formerly guided by general mission statements that could not be easily translated into action. Specialized goals should lead department members to ask, "How can we work to accomplish that goal?" The answers may range from community education programs to directed patrol strategies to improved communication with the public.

Before developing strategies to meet these goals, administrators should be cognizant of some established facts within the field of policing and criminal justice. Recognition and understanding of these facts will prevent today's administrators from falling into common historical pitfalls that continue to direct patrol strategies today. They also challenge some common myths related to policing strategies.

Myth #1:   Random patrol prevents crime and reduces fear of crime.

Many people believe that random patrol prevents crime and reduces fear of crime among citizens. As the Kansas City Preventative Patrol Experiment illustrated, increasing or decreasing the number of patrol units in a geographic area has little effect on the crime rate or on fear of crime *(Kelling, 1974)*. Despite this landmark study, random patrol and rapid response continues to be the most common patrol tactic used by departments today. Progressive departments need to move away from this traditional patrol method and should embrace alternate proactive and preventative strategies that will have a long-lasting impact on crime.

Myth #2:   Officers are busy and have no spare time.

A 2005 study revealed that between 70 – 79% of a police officer's shift can be characterized as downtime *(Famega, 2005)*. Although certain times of day or days of the week may be busier than others, officers do have spare time that could be better used. Encouraging officers to use this time differently and more productively may be a challenge but in the end officers may find that the expanded activities that they engage in are extremely rewarding and contribute to their improved morale.

Myth #3:   Response time should be the highest priority.

Another very popular myth is that speed counts. Officers often activate their blue lights and sirens to get to calls quickly, when in reality fast response times rarely impact the outcome of the majority of calls for service. Many calls are not time sensitive and the proximity of mobile patrol units has little outcome on the result of the call.

Myth #4:   A city can be evenly divided into patrol sectors by equally dividing the geographic areas.

Police leaders may believe that communities can be easily divided into geographic locations based on size. Because every city or town has specific areas that have different needs, shift commanders should take the time to contemplate personnel deployment and patrol strategies. Rural residential areas may require little attention, while busy downtown commercial districts may benefit from park and walks or bike patrol officers in addition to the traditional officer driving through in a cruiser.

> **Myth #5: Police administrators have little effect on employee morale.**
>
> It is false to assume that employee morale cannot be directed or controlled. While morale levels will constantly fluctuate, administrators and the rank and file can have a substantial impact on the work environment. Attending training and reading up on improving the workplace can help employees best understand the nature of the work environment and how to make it the best that it can be.

Since the inception of community policing in the 1980s, a great deal of law enforcement has remained the same and much has changed. Entering into a new millennium and a new Era with evolving challenges should inspire some police executives to re-evaluate the focus of their agencies. While mission statements and general directives have guided police policy in the past, the use of specific and articulate goals based on this new agency assessment will help every department create tangible strategies to best respond to the ever-changing needs of their communities.

End Notes

Famega, C. N. (2005). Variation in officer downtime: A review of the research. *Policing: An International Journal of Police Strategies and Management*, 28(3), 388–414. Bingley, United Kingdom: Emerald Group Publishing Limited.

Hench, D. (2006, January 4). To be able to compete, Maine police simplify recruit process. Portland Press Herald. p. A1.

Kelling, G. L., Pate, A. M., Dieckman, D., & Brown, C. (1974). *The Kansas City preventative patrol experiment: Technical report.* Washington, DC: Police Foundation.

A frequent complaint of police supervisors today is the struggle they face managing the new generation of workers. They have been confused by, and at times frustrated with, the characteristics of this generation. Traditional supervisory and training strategies are failing, resulting in both the supervisors and subordinates feeling frustrated and misunderstood. This is an ongoing cycle as each generation is forced to deal with the perplexing attributes of the younger generation.

There is good news. If police supervisors take the time to understand these workers by learning about the type of supervision that they require and the work environment that they will thrive in, they will have the ability to better manage this workforce. This, ultimately, will result in an appreciation for the many significant contributions that this generation has to offer and an overall improvement in the quality of service that the police department is able to provide.

Defining the Millennial Generation

The Millennials, also referred to as Generation Y, were born between 1978 and the late 1990s. They currently make up the bulk of applicants and existing patrol officers, as older officers move up through the ranks or retire. Like generations before them, members of the Millennial generation have been shaped and formed by significant political, social and economic events that occurred during their childhood and adolescence. Notably, the Millennials experienced the Reagan, Clinton and Bush presidencies. They were teenagers during the rise of gang and drug violence in the 1990s. They have watched the increase of concern regarding environmental issues such as global warming, pollution and the inevitable end of critical resources. They watched two teenagers open fire inside a Colorado high school and experienced a heightened focus on school safety and security.

They watched the World Trade Center towers crumble and watched the United States initiate wars in Afghanistan and Iraq. It's hard for them to remember life without the Internet, text messaging, Facebook, ebay, Google, On Demand, cable television and cell phones. They grew up watching "reality" television which transitioned to interactive television programs such as American Idol.

In addition to watching these significant events unfold around them, the Millennials were parented unlike any generation before them. Parents placed a heavy focus on their children and on child-rearing. They were doting parents, sometimes referred to as "helicopter parents" due to their constant hovering, who wanted to protect their children from any physical or emotional pain. They were exposed to great diversity and were provided with a multitude of opportunities. They were told they could do anything and that everything they did was great. They are sometimes referred to as "trophy kids" because everyone was a winner and everyone got a trophy or a blue ribbon regardless of their performance. This practice sheltered them from ever experiencing what it feels like to fail. They were given many opportunities to participate in sports, social activities, music and community events. They lead busy, scheduled and structured lives. They adjusted to frequent change, new challenges and new opportunities. They were accustomed to constantly being told that they were doing a great job and thrived on high levels of praise and feedback.

These experiences growing up shaped the current generation of incoming workers. Although it is not fair to say that every member of a generation possesses these characteristics, many do. Understanding common Millennial traits and their origins will help police supervisors be better able to coach and lead these individuals.

Millennial Characteristics

Like the generations before them, these workers have specific characteristics that define who they are. In general, they are a group of optimistic, self-inventive, creative, multi-taskers who need constant praise, feedback and access to new opportunities. They are educated and intelligent. They are technologically savvy and are less likely to shy away from new computer software or other equipment. This flexibility extends beyond technology as they do not resist change as much as the older generations. An extension of these characteristics are certain preferences and expectations regarding their work environment and career.

Millennial Expectations—Advancement

These workers often have a strong sense of entitlement. Veteran officers remember "putting their time in" on the midnight shift or working other less than desirable assignments. They understood that it takes time to be offered special assignments, to be trusted, to be respected and, certainly, to be promoted. The Millennials do not have this same belief. When surveyed about their expectations at their jobs regarding advancement, over half (51%) indicated that they expected to advance in 1 – 2 years. Another 19% expect advancement in 2 – 3 years *(Robert Half International, 2008)*. This is a significant challenge for police administrators who recognize that opportunities for special assignment and promotion are often few and far between.

However, there are ways to meet these needs. Supervisors can create new positions of responsibility or task forces that are designed to deal with specific issues. These may not be promotional opportunities, but if the positions are interesting, involve an increased level of responsibility and are challenging, Millennials may find that these assignments meet some of their needs for advancement while they wait for more traditional opportunities to become available. Examples of these types of assignments would include the formation of Neighborhood Watch groups, Warrant Apprehension Squads, proactive patrol groups that focus on one specific issue (such as a recent rash of car breaks or noise complaints), accreditation teams, in-house training instructors or a myriad of other activities. Creative thinking administrators may be able to identify specific tasks that will meet the problem-solving and social needs of the Millennial officer, while also responding to identified community needs.

Millennial Expectations—Supervisory Contact

Unlike the generations before them, Millennials prefer a high level of supervisory contact. Where Baby Boomers wanted to avoid the boss altogether and Generation X employees wanted consistent and predictable contact, the Millennials seek frequent daily contact. According to one study only 10% of Millennials feel comfortable with weekly contact with their bosses, while the majority (35%) prefer daily feedback *(Robert Half International, 2008)*.

Millennials also prefer a supervisory style that is quite different than the traditional, quasi-military style that so many police departments are accustomed to. Because of this, rigid hierarchical structures may have to be flexible to accommodate these new workers. When Millennials were surveyed about the desired characteristics in their dream boss, they were identified as:

- Good management skills

- Pleasant and easy to get along with

- Understanding and caring

- Flexible and open-minded

- Respects/values/appreciates employees

- Good communication skills
(Robert Half International, 2008)

The same survey asked respondents to rank the most important factors in their work environments. Working with a manager that they can respect and learn from was ranked number one *(Robert Half International, 2008)*. Their second choice was working with people that they enjoy.

As these survey results indicate, the Millennials are an extremely sociable generation. They value family, friends and positive personal contacts. In fact, two-thirds of the respondents in this survey indicated that they prefer in-person communication with co-workers instead of email or other less personal means of communication *(Robert Half International, 2008)*.

Successful supervisors will make an effort to have frequent, informal contacts with employees. They should have an open-door policy to make it clear that they are approachable. They must role model appropriate behavior and treat peers and subordinates with respect. They should also strive to assist subordinates with professional development and growth. They will be looking for supervisors to guide and coach them through their individual careers so that they can gain new responsibilities and work toward promotion.

Millennial Expectations—Fairness

A strong characteristic of Millennial employees is their focus on fairness. They were brought up by doting parents who heavily emphasized fairness. The challenge is that sometimes things aren't fair. This is a difficult lesson for these individuals who may feel frustrated and angry at perceived favoritism or poor decision-making. Additionally, they feel completely confident talking openly about it. This is not a generation that keeps feelings to themselves. They were taught to speak out and speak up. Millennials are likely to approach peers and supervisors with complaints about workplace fairness issues.

The best supervisory response to complaints of fairness is to be approachable and to listen to the employees' concerns. This is said with caution, as supervisors are not a sounding board for excessive complaining and whining. However, employees should be given an opportunity to voice their concerns and need to feel that they have been heard and that their opinion is valued. Ultimately, however, the best response is to stand by the original decision, explain the reasons for it (if appropriate) and to then send the employee on his or her way. Millennials need to feel that they can voice their concerns. If they do not have this opportunity, they will become frustrated, may develop resentment, may not feel valued and may start looking for a new employer.

Millennial Expectations—Community/Global Perspective

Members of this generation have grown up with a dramatically increased world view when compared to generations before them. Advances in technology have allowed them to read about and watch world events unfolding in real time. They also have the ability to engage, via technology, with individuals worldwide. They can go online and, within seconds, be "chatting" with someone from almost anywhere on the globe. For these reasons, the Millennials are keenly aware of world events. This, in combination with their high social needs, has made them a fairly caring generation. They value workplaces that have these same values. While they want to be cared for individually, through good salary, benefits and retirement packages, they also want their employer to be socially responsible on a local and even global level. This concern is illustrated by Andre Brown, a Millennial respondent of the Robert Half International Survey, when she stated, "The companies that stand out the most are those that provide for their employees and their community just as much as they provide for their customers." *(p.5)* The nature of police work is inherently connected to serving the community, but keeping this Millennial value in mind reinforces the value of outreach programs that emphasize improved quality of life, volunteerism and public service.

Millennial employees present many challenges for existing supervisors who may not be familiar with the unique needs of this new generation. They are impatient and expect and desire immediate rewards. They lack experience, yet feel entitled to respect and new assignments. They are over-confident in their abilities and may take action in unfamiliar situations without seeking guidance from a seasoned veteran officer. They respect people based on personal relationships rather than on the formal hierarchy. They may question authority and feel comfortable vocalizing their personal opinions and complaints. They pay close attention to issues of fairness and equality and are quick to speak up if they perceive favoritism and poor decision-making. They seek upward mobility quickly and will seek change if they do not see a new path to promotion or new assignment in the near future. They can easily lose interest in their jobs and will become bored more quickly than employees from generations past.

Millennial workers can be high-risk and high-maintenance, but they have the capacity to be exceptional employees, if they are placed in the right environment.

The best environment will be supportive of some or all of the following desires of the Millennials:

- To be coached and lead, rather than told and ordered

- To be challenged, thus avoiding boredom

- To have a fun and relaxed workplace, rather than a formal one

- To be respected by their peers and supervisors, rather than disregarded as inexperienced

- To work with optimists instead of pessimists

- To learn new things and be stimulated

- To make a good salary

- To see a short and clear path to new opportunities and advancement

- To have room for creative expression and to have their ideas heard and considered

- To have variety in their daily tasks

- To have established and reachable goals

Coincidentally, one of the best ways to keep Millennial employees interested in their jobs, and ultimately to retain them, is to offer them new responsibilities and opportunities that will challenge and stimulate them. Society today has expanded expectations of their police force and Millennial employees may thrive fulfilling their basic patrol function as well as these evolving challenges. These new tasks emphasize creative problem solving and citizen contact and may be the perfect fit for this new generation of workers.

End Notes

Robert Half International and Yahoo! HotJobs. (2008). *What Millennial workers want: How to attract and retain generation Y employees.* RHI-0308-0056. Menlo Park, CA.

C hief, deputy chief, captain, lieutenant, sergeant, field training officer—there are a lot of supervisory roles on a police department. The majority of these individuals have worked their way up through the ranks with little or no formal education in the area of administration and leadership and perhaps minimal departmental training that address these issues. Before writing new policies, implementing new programs or changing deployment tactics, it is imperative that these supervisors have a solid understanding of leadership and management theory.

Manager versus Leader

Prior to entering into this discussion, one must first recognize the difference between a manager and a leader. Within a police department, a lieutenant can be a manager but not a leader and likewise, an officer can be a leader but not a manager. Quite simply, a manager is someone that is assigned to a superior position and makes decisions that impact those working within his/her span of control. Leaders, on the other hand, can exist anywhere within an agency. Leaders gain their influence not through formal assignment but most often from the respect and admiration of their peers. It has been said that some people are born leaders; they were organizing games of tag on the playground when they were five years old, while the other children followed their lead.

This distinction between managers and leaders is important when considering implementing any change. For example, when adding a new program, it is critical to recognize and gain the support of the informal leaders within a department. This is, arguably, more important than allying with titled managers.

Contemporary Leadership Styles

Implementing change in the daily operations of a police department or in the written policies and procedures simply will not work if the transition is not well-managed by effective leaders who value communication. In this new era and with the new Millennial employees, supervisors need to be realistic about the limitations of the traditional police hierarchy and rigid leadership styles. More contemporary management styles are required. There is a lot of research in this vast field. Countless studies and books have been published that identify and explain new-age management theory. The most notable pieces of these theories emphasize free flowing communication and attention to customer satisfaction.

While the importance of good communication is an issue that has hopefully already been contemplated by progressive administrators and executives, the concept of customer satisfaction may be a fairly foreign term. Although the private business world and the public sector vary in many ways, the basics of management, leadership and motivation have strong parallels that can greatly benefit a police agency. The truth is, private businesses often have the luxury of being able to spend money to explore these matters whether it is through private consultants, training or research projects. Public sector managers usually don't have this luxury and can instead learn by watching. Successful businesses use a variety of different models that steer leadership strategies, managerial communication, the promotional process, employee morale and assess many other psychological and sociological issues within the workplace. The focus on customer satisfaction has been a growing trend in the business world and that trend has been mirrored in the world of law enforcement through the emphasis on community policing.

While community policing prioritizes a customer-focused philosophy, that emphasis has not necessarily resonated to management personnel. This is most likely due to the long history of a rigid, quasi-military hierarchy that dominates the field of policing. When community policing was first introduced dramatic changes to the hierarchical structure were acknowledged, but not emphasized. Words such as "decentralized" and "mini chiefs" were included in early community policing concepts, but new management techniques were not clearly articulated. Instead, the focus was on community partnerships and problem solving at the officer level. This has left an existing command structure that stifles creativity, limits individual variation and works within the confines of outdated policing strategies. This is not satisfying to community members because it does not value the "customer." Despite the well-established hierarchy and resistance to change, it is important to examine private sector contemporary management models and apply them to police administration so that there is a new focus on "customer" needs.

There are a wide variety of new management models that all have their own strengths and weaknesses. Many of these strategies have been successfully implemented in businesses worldwide. The following section identifies some popular contemporary management concepts.

Reengineering the Corporation

Reengineering the corporation involves the complete overhaul and redesign of the internal workings of an agency. Using this technique administrators are challenged to envision starting the entire department or business from scratch. In their influential book on this topic Michael Hammer and James Champy define this term as "… the fundamental rethinking and radical redesign of business process to achieve dramatic improvements in critical, contemporary measures of performance, such as cost, quality of service and speed" *(1993, p. 32)*. The goal is to reduce bureaucracy and to improve efficiency. So many departments are what they are today because of their history. Police departments started as hierarchical, reactive units with a primary focus on law enforcement and criminal apprehension. But, if these agencies were to be completely destroyed and had to be rebuilt and redesigned, what would they look like? How many of the standard operating procedures of today's police agency would be kept and how many would be abandoned as archaic and ineffective? These are the fundamental questions of using the reengineering the corporation concept.

Management by Walking Around

Management By Walking Around or Management By Wandering Around (MBWA) is a fairly simple concept. Administrators and executives practice this technique by leaving their offices and by walking around the workplace interacting with subordinates. It is a hands-on approach that encourages casual communication and direct participation by executives. It requires that managers have good listening skills and good interpersonal communication skills. Using this technique can empower street-level employees by allowing them to feel heard and having their opinions valued. It can help to reduce the "us-versus-them" attitude between the officers and those in rank. If this technique is used, managers should be careful to avoid picking and choosing favorites whom they engage with. Every employee should be treated equally and should feel included in this process to avoid feeling ostracized or ignored. The use of MBWA is often informally practiced by some supervisors who have a natural understanding of the importance of staying connected with all members of an agency.

Total Quality Management

Total Quality Management (TQM) is based on consistency and customer satisfaction. The theory is that most problems can be ironed out through efficiency by reducing variation and ensuring that things are done correctly the first time, every time. Managers aggressively work toward reducing defects and waste from every section of operations. Quality assurance specialists may be put into place to guarantee that these goals are met and to come up with solutions if they are not. In conjunction with efficient production, TQM emphasizes the collection of feedback from the customer to evaluate the quality of the services rendered.

The use of TQM in the business world is perhaps easier to envision than in the world of policing. A factory that produces a particular product can more easily be broken down into clear and definitive sections that can be individually assessed and controlled. If a problem is identified with the product, a manager can simply go to where that problem occurred and work toward fixing it. The world of policing is a bit more complicated with a wide variety of unpredictability and individual variation. Not only are so many calls for service slightly different than the next, but every officer incorporates his own individual beliefs and ethics into his discretionary decision-making. The ability of each officer to use her discretion makes the TQM process challenging to implement. However, it is not impossible. For example, managers can ensure that every time officers respond to a domestic violence call, all parties are offered a restraining order, all parties are given references to contact and a police report is always completed. There is no guarantee that two officers will always respond, that charges will always be filed or that officers will handle the interpersonal communication in a standardized way. Because of the inherent unpredictable nature of police work, these types of guarantees are not practical and would be impossible to use as measurements of success. However, identifying best practices and attainable goals to achieve desired outcomes is a reasonable objective and one that would fall under the concept of TQM *(Special Focus 7.1)*.

If an administrator were to use the TQM management style, it would require the review of each different type of call and the best response in ideal conditions. That response can then be incorporated into established policies and procedures that would guide officers and street-level supervisors as they make their decisions.

This book provides a quick peek into management and leadership issues. There are many resources available to further explore these important ideas. Books, college courses and training will enhance a person's understanding of these concepts. The brief overview of these different techniques should reveal that many of these strategies may already be employed, even if it is on an informal basis. That is because a lot of contemporary management theory is based in common sense and natural human tendencies. Theorists didn't just sit down and create these far-fetched theories. Instead, they watched work environments and existing managers to see what worked. In that way, management theory is simply a reflection of what already works. Familiarizing managers with these theories will provide support for those who already practice them and will introduce new and effective ideas to those who do not.

Special Focus 7.1: Example: Total Quality Management Put into Practice

Total Quality Management (TQM) places an emphasis on ensuring that a business or agency produces a quality service or product in an efficient and consistent manner. This concept is easily visualized in the business world, where tangible products, such as cars, are built at a production center. Each employee has a different job and problems can be isolated to a specific step in the process. Once identified, the problem can be studied and eventually remedied to improve quality. Beyond the manufacturing plant, customers who visit dealerships and who eventually purchase vehicles are asked about their satisfaction with both the service they received and the product itself. This management strategy includes "the big picture." Perhaps surprisingly, this same tactic can be applied to policing.

Although police perform many activities, most can be placed into categories such as processing crime scenes, conducting motor vehicle stops, pursuit driving or responding to motor vehicle accidents. Each type of activity can and should be reviewed to identify the best practice. Responding to motor vehicle accidents is a good example. This process can be broken down from its inception to its conclusion and each part can be assessed to determine if it is efficient and effective. The following is an example of how TQM could be applied to police response to motor vehicle collisions:

Training: Though it may seem far removed, training is the first step in most of what police officers do on the job. *Do all officers receive the same training regarding motor vehicle response? Is that training the best that it can be? Does it reflect current practices?*

Policy: Policies should guide an officer's behavior. Consequently, poorly written or outdated policies will result in inadequate responses. *Is the policy thorough? Is it updated? Does it reflect changes in law? Is it reasonable?*

Police Response: Most managers who do not practice TQM would start their assessment of the event at this phase. *How was the officer's response? Did the officer conform to written policies? Was a citation issued? Was the scene cleared in a timely manner? How was traffic handled during the accident? Did the various responding agencies work well together on the scene? Was the equipment that the officer had adequate?*

Written Reports: Once the scene has been cleared officers must then complete the associated paperwork. *Was the on-scene investigation thorough and complete? Did the officer complete the report in a timely manner? Were all the appropriate forms completed? Were the forms forwarded to the correct locations?*

Customer Satisfaction: Commonly overlooked in the field of policing is the element of customer satisfaction. This information can provide an insightful perspective that may improve police practices. Some departments mail out random surveys to people who have had police contact, such as the drivers and occupants involved in motor vehicle collisions, to inquire about the quality of the police services that they received.

Communication with Outside Agencies: In many cases, multiple agencies respond to the same events that police are called to. A motor vehicle collision will sometimes require police, fire, EMS, a utility company and a tow truck company. Dispatch centers are almost always involved in police activity. Communication and coordination among these agencies is imperative and reaching out to other agency representatives is an excellent way to engage in TQM.

As this example illustrates, TQM is applicable to policing. It takes time and commitment, but should result in an improved quality of service and better cross-agency and community relations.

An interesting side note about police managers is that they rarely have any significant amount of formal training in the areas of management, leadership and motivation. Yet, they are in critically important positions to direct employees and to establish/maintain a positive workplace environment. This is especially true with first-line supervisors, often sergeants, who work side by side with officers. They are the middlemen between officers and upper-level executives and may be the employees who have the most impact on morale, employee development and quality of services. Yet, in most cases, those promoted are people who never set out to be managers. They are those that performed well as officers, did well in the promotional process and who may or may not have leadership skills. They are then promoted and find themselves in the unfamiliar world of management. It is for this reason that significant management training should be incorporated into the promotional process so that these newly minted supervisors can transition away from their prior duties as police officers and into their new duties as supervisors.

The Peter Principle

The term Peter Principle was first identified in 1969 in a book written by Dr. Laurence J. Peter and Raymond Hull. It refers to the process of promoting a person to their highest level of incompetence. The argument is that people get promoted for excelling at a job. They will continue this process as they work their way up through the ranks and perform well. When they stop performing well and are unable to accomplish their duties successfully, they are not promoted. Instead, they are left to finish out their careers in positions in which they fail. Recognition of this principle and how it happens can be a useful tidbit for police managers who should strive to avoid having a department filled with people working unsuccessfully in their positions. To avoid this promotional pitfall, it is important to choose employees for promotion not based solely on their current success, but instead on a combination of their current success and their predicted capacity to do well at the new position. Because every position within an agency can vary so much from another, moving people into new positions should be done with careful deliberation and consideration. The question should not be, "Are they doing well at what they do?" Instead the question should be, "Do they have the capacity and personal characteristics to do well in the new position?"

The Dilbert Principle

The Dilbert Principle was first identified by the Dilbert cartoonist Scott Adams in the 1990s. This theory suggests that employees who fail to thrive, are inept and who may negatively affect the overall performance of an organization are sometimes promoted to positions where they will do less harm to the organization as a whole. These individuals may find themselves in middle-management where it is theorized that they can do the least amount of harm. In one Dilbert cartoon written in 1995 that addresses this issue, the lead character Dogbert states, "... leadership is nature's way of removing morons from the productive flow." Although Adams initially touched on this theory in a daily comic strip, the concept quickly caught on and he went on to write a book which has become popular in leadership and management curriculums at colleges and universities *(1997)*.

Characteristics of a Good Supervisor

Choosing managers can be a challenging process. There are many different issues to consider. There is no one right personality type that will make the best manager. Many different types of people work successfully as managers and are able to lead subordinates. Anyone who has ever worked on a police department can usually recall a wide variety of supervisors, all with their own strengths and weaknesses. Some managers may be more friendly and informal, while others may be more rigid and cold. Some may emphasize arrest and apprehension and others may emphasize community services and working toward long-term solutions. In addition to supervisory variation, individual employees respond differently to varying personality types. Diversity within employees provides a workforce that is able to best meet the ever-growing demands of a community.

**Whatever his individual personality,
a good manager does the following:**

- Role-models appropriate behavior

- Supports new ideas and creativity

- Seeks improvement

- Inspires change

- Communicates organizational goals and the overall vision of the agency

- Understands customer satisfaction

- Encourages collaboration to solve problems

- Maintains positive attitude and optimism

- Stays highly visible and stays actively involved

- Brings forth new ideas

Good leaders and managers are hard to find. From a practical standpoint, police chiefs are often limited in what they have to choose from. Stringent hiring and promotion rules may prevent the best candidates from being selected. But there is sometimes room for choice. When that choice is made and individuals are chosen for certain positions, it is important that these characteristics are considered so that the person who is the right fit is awarded the position *(Special Focus 7.2)*. This strategy emphasizes positive, optimistic and forward thinkers to be promoted above others who may have more seniority or more diverse experience. The ultimate issue is finding an individual who will best fit into the job. Seniority and experience should not be the primary factors considered. Police administrators are strongly encouraged to focus on a long-term vision for the department by making selections for promotions and special assignments based on personal character and potential. Once managers are promoted they should be educated in contemporary leadership and management strategies with an emphasis on customer satisfaction. This preparation will turn managers into leaders who will carry a department forward in this new era.

Special Focus 7.2:   Selecting the Best: How to Select Personnel for Promotion and Special Assignment

One of the most challenging duties of any police administrator is the selection of personnel for promotion and special assignments. It is imperative that great attention and diligence be paid to this process to ensure the future success of an organization. But what tools should administrators use to determine who should be selected? Traditionally police departments have relied heavily on seniority and written exam scores. While experience and good test-taking skills are respectable, they should not be the only factors used in selection. Police administrators should consider some of the following standards to measure an employee's potential ability to be successful in a new position:

- **Performance evaluations:** Police administrators should ensure that every member of an agency is reviewed every six months or every year. These written evaluations should be standardized and should be completed by supervisors who work closely with the employee. Employee evaluations should include basic duties, but should also include recommendations for future assignments. These evaluations should provide administrators with a detailed and thorough review of an employee's performance over time and should identify potential leaders.

- **Sick time use:** It is recommended that this information be used cautiously, as it would be unfair to punish people who have taken extended periods of time off for the birth of a child, childcare, surgery or major illness. However, generalized patterns of calling out could be a sign of an apathetic employee and one who could negatively contribute to the overall environment of the workplace.

- **Self-initiated activity:** The best leaders do not require constant direction. They can identify problems and work toward solutions. Historically, arrest statistics and motor vehicle citation numbers were the most prominent measures of officer-initiated activity. While excelling in these areas does show initiative, it is equally important to consider other areas of activity as well. Officers that bring new technologies into the work place, identify and run new programs, work toward updating and writing policy, engage in community meetings, initiate positive citizen contacts or who work on long-term goals should be recognized as well. These traits are just as valuable as the traditional measurements of activity.

- **Recommendations from supervisors and officers:** While certain individuals may look great on paper, personal discussions with those that work with the employee may reveal a surplus of problems that had gone undetected. As simple as this step seems, it can be easily overlooked. Take the time to talk with coworkers in a private and professional manner in order to determine that applicant's true qualifications for the vacant position.

While an employee's past history and job performance is important, her potential capacity and predicted ability to succeed in the new position should be the primary considerations. It is a common pitfall to focus on years of service or who is "next in line." Using this strategy to promote is ineffective and will have dramatic long-term negative effects on the department overall. Individuals who are selected for promotional positions and special assignments will be the future leaders of a department. Individuals who are optimistic, creative, forward-thinking, open-minded, hard-working, committed to the vision of the department, honest and who have a history of effective problem-solving should be an agency's next leaders.

Source: Kasper, J. (2010). The right fit: Choosing the best people for promotion and special assignments. *The Police Chief Magazine*, Volume 77, Number 9, pages 70-71.

End Notes

Adams, S. (1997). *The Dilbert principle: A cubicle's-eye view of bosses, meetings, management fads & other workplace afflictions.* New York: Harper Paperbacks.

Hammer, M., & Champy, J. (1993). *Reengineering the Corporation: A manifesto for business revolution.* New York: Harper Collins.

Kasper, J. (2010). The Right Fit: Choosing the Best People for Promotion and Special Assignments. *The Police Chief Magazine*, Volume 77, Number 9, pages 70-71.

Peter, L. J., & Hull, R. (1969). *The Peter Principle: Why things always go wrong.* New York: William Morrow and Company.

While two separate police officers may carry the same title, wear similar uniforms or perform similar daily duties, there can be dramatic differences between their agencies. These differences are often based on the population of the community that is served. An agency's size can easily range from two or three officers to over five hundred. Although large city police departments do attract a lot of attention, the majority of agencies in the United States are quite small. A 2004 Bureau of Justice Statistics survey reported that 23.6% of departments have 10 – 24 full-time officers, 19.7% have 5 – 9 full-time officers and 18.4% have 2 – 4 full-time officers *(DOJ, 2007, p. 2)*. Consequently almost 62% of all police departments in the U.S. have between 2 and 24 full-time officers. The smaller the agency, the more diverse each employee's duties will be. The employees in these small agencies must balance fiscal management, community relations, investigations, training, personnel management and response to calls for service. For example, a large department may have one officer specifically committed to public relations, while personnel from smaller agencies will have media relations as one of many administrative duties.

Regardless of size, every police department must handle diverse administrative duties that keep an agency running. These behind-the-scenes assignments should not be overlooked when considering successful policing strategies. Without people focusing on the logistics and details, there would be no uniforms, no cruisers, no buildings, no training, no policies, no recruiting and no hiring.

Administrative Duties

Although the quantity of administrative duties is far too lengthy to list (as any police administrator would agree), there are specific tasks that are strongly connected to the success or failure of effective policing strategies *(Special Focus 8.1)*. These tasks include: accreditation, establishing minimum qualification standards, recruitment and hiring, training, employee evaluation and technology.

Special Focus 8.1: **Administrative Duties: East Brunswick, New Jersey Police Department**

The duties of a police Administrative Division can easily be forgotten, as officers and citizens alike tend to focus on the activities of the uniformed patrol division or the detective bureau. However, without great attention to detail to the behind the scenes operations of a police agency, no one would be able to do their jobs safely and effectively. Although the duties that fall under the Administrative Commander may vary slightly from agency to agency, employees working in these sections generally handle many of the same duties. The following list details the functions of the Administrative Division of the East Brunswick, New Jersey Police Department.

The Administrative Division oversees the operation of the following functions:

- Coordination and daily oversight of the Department of Public Safety's budget
- Police Records Bureau
- Departmental computer operations
- Fleet management
- Police communication services and civilian dispatchers
- Purchasing, payroll, and quasi-duty administration
- Alarm ordinance enforcement
- Operations of the east Brunswick Police Training Facility
- Operations of the Departmental Training Officer and coordination of all departmental training
- Operations of the East Brunswick Police Community Policing Unit

- Recruitment and hiring of all sworn and civilian employees for the Department of Public Safety
- Coordination of pre-employment background investigations of potential employees
- Oversight of the Office of Professional Standards
- Policy Development
- Internal Affairs
- Promotional Process

Reprinted with permission from Captain William Krause, Jr., East Brunswick, NJ PD.

Accreditation

The application of accreditation to policing began at the end of the turbulent 1970s. After decades of working toward police reform, the development of the Commission on Accreditation for Law Enforcement Agencies, Inc. (CALEA®) was established in 1979. According to CALEA's® website, "The purpose of CALEA's® Accreditation Programs is to improve the delivery of public safety services, primarily by: maintaining a body of standards, developed by public safety practitioners, covering a wide range of up-to-date public safety initiatives; establishing and administering an accreditation process; and recognizing professional excellence (CALEA®)." The pursuit of accreditation is completely voluntary. Agencies that do work toward this certification must meet a specific number of mandatory standards in different areas and must also meet a certain percentage of other-than-mandatory standards. The number of standards that must be met will vary by agency based on size and function. There is an enrollment fee and a yearly fee associated with the process through CALEA®. Current yearly fees range from $3,300 to $5,600 and are based on an agency's number of authorized full-time employees, both sworn and non-sworn. (CALEA®).

Reprinted with permission from Janice Dixon.

The value of accreditation has been a hotly debated topic. There are those strongly committed to both sides of the argument.

When considering accreditation, it is important to be aware of both the advantages and disadvantages of the program.

According to CALEA's® website and reading materials, the major advantages of accreditation are:

• Greater accountability within the agency

• Reduced risk and liability exposure

• Stronger defense against civil law suits

• Consistent support from government officials

• Increased community advocacy

There are other advantages associated with accreditation as well. In most cases, accreditation will inspire a move toward more state of the art technology. This may include changes in radio and communication systems, computer software upgrades or new programs, surveillance cameras in cruisers or within a station for enhanced building security and prisoner monitoring. There will also be paperwork and task improvement that will result in more efficient use of time. These changes, as well as many others that occur during the accreditation process, will increase departmental pride and morale, which should be reflected in improved performance and community relationships.

Despite these significant advantages associated with accreditation, there are disadvantages as well:

• **Money:** Aside from the yearly fee, the process requires an enormous amount of work hours.

• **Time and effort:** Employees who work toward accreditation will have less time for other projects and small agencies may not have the personnel available to commit to this task.

- **Resentment from police administrators:** They may believe that their agency is already efficient and running smoothly.

- **Resentment from unions and individual employees:** They may resist change and see it as a change in working conditions and that they are being asked to participate in tasks that are not "real" police work.

On a national level, police administrators seem to be slowly grabbing onto the idea of accreditation. Trends show a gradual increase in the number of newly minted accredited police agencies across the country. In an interview with Janice Dixon, the Program Specialist for CALEA®, she indicated that 1999 marked the 20th anniversary of CALEA®. At that time, there were 532 law enforcement agencies accredited through their organization. As of 2009, that number increased to 590 accredited agencies, with 154 agencies in the self-assessment phase and pursuing formal accreditation *(J. Dixon, personal communication, September 28, 2009).* It appears that this trend will persist as agencies work toward professionalization.

In addition to CALEA®, some states also have accreditation commissions. Departments can pursue accreditation through either the national or state certifying agencies. For those administrators who have considered this process, it can be a daunting task. However, accreditation commissions are aware that the process may seem intimidating or overwhelming to police employees who are charged with this task. Therefore, they have excellent reading materials, training and on-line information that clearly articulate each step of the process *(Special Focus 8.2).*

Special Focus 8.2: Becoming Accredited: A Five-Step Process

There are five steps to the accreditation process.

First step: Agencies begin by sending personnel to informational training. They will receive documents and handouts on the accreditation process and they will need to thoroughly review those readings. It is helpful during the early phase of accreditation to visit other police departments that are accredited and to talk with personnel who worked toward that goal. Personnel should then begin reviewing internal policies and standards. This step is by far the most time-consuming, as every single policy and procedure must be reviewed and sometimes adjusted. Many agencies may learn that they do not have policies that are mandatory and they will need to write them. Pieces of equipment may be outdated or inoperable. Personnel may be unfamiliar with standard operating procedures. Training certificates may have expired. All of these issues must be remedied before the agency can move on.

Second step: Complete a self-assessment. The standards that the review panel will be looking for are clearly laid out and employees can conduct a mock assessment before the formal one to ensure that everything is in place.

Third step: The on-site assessment. This involves assessors from the accreditation commission doing an on-site check of the building, in-house facilities and fleet. It also entails a rigorous review of policies and procedures and employee interactions in the form of random questions about departmental rules and procedures.

Fourth step: The commission's review and decision. Once on-site assessors have completed their review, they make recommendations to the commission regarding whether or not the agency has met the required standards. If they have, the commission will usually grant accreditation.

Fifth step: The maintenance of compliance and the re-accreditation process that occurs once every three years.

Source: www.calea.org

Minimum Hiring Standards—Education

Whether or not an agency seeks accreditation, it must engage in the process of recruitment and candidate selection. However, before improving recruitment strategies, administrators will be responsible for determining minimum hiring standards for police candidates. These usually involve a state driver's license, the ability to swim, a clean criminal record and a clean driving record. Beyond these qualifications, candidates must also pass psychological exams, fitness tests, a criminal background check and an interview panel. The question that has been contested regarding the minimum qualifications of police officers is that of education. According to a 2003 Bureau of Justice Statistics survey, 98% of agencies have some form of educational requirement *(DOJ, 2003, p. 9)*. Out of those, 81% require a high school diploma, 8% require some college, 9% require a two-year college degree and 1% require a four-year degree *(2003, p. 9)*. There has been an ongoing trend over the past few decades to hire officers that have college degrees and/or to support officers in their quest to obtain college degrees once hired *(Table 8.1)*. Many agencies reward officers for their education levels by paying college-educated officers more or by having educational incentive programs.

The push toward college-educated police officers and the resulting tax dollars spent on supporting these programs has resulted in a battle between fiscally strapped local and state governments and police administrators who believe in these programs. This conflict has inspired researchers to explore the subject in an effort to provide some finality to this conflict. The results are overwhelmingly clear: on average officers with formal college educations have many advantages over their peers. Dr. Rebecca Paynich completed a thorough review of the research on this subject in her paper, "The Impact of a College-Educated Police Force: A Review of the Literature." In this paper Paynich identifies the following attributes of college-educated officers *(2009)*:

- Have better communication skills

- Write better reports

- Are more tolerant with citizens

- Display clearer thinking

- Have a better understanding of policing and the criminal justice system

- Have a better comprehension of civil rights issues from multiple perspectives

- Adapt better to organizational change

- Are more professional

- Have fewer administrative and personnel problems

- Are better able to utilize innovative techniques

- Receive fewer citizen complaints

- Receive fewer disciplinary actions

- Have fewer preventable accidents

- Take less sick time away from work

- Perform better in police training

- Are less likely to use deadly force

- Are less cynical

- Are more open-minded

- Place a higher value on ethical conduct

In general, college-educated officers bring more to the table based on their experience in the world of academia. In addition to learning the facts of their subject area, they develop enhanced skills in writing, communication, preparation, time management, problem solving, creativity, empathy, flexibility and decision-making. They also incur a few more years of life experience before becoming police officers. Agencies that are seeking candidates who will excel in the new era of policing should absolutely be seeking college graduates.

Table 8.1: Bureau of Justice Table: Minimum educational requirements for new officers in local police departments, by size of population served, 2003

Population served	Total with requirement	High school diploma	Some college	2-year college degree	4-year college degree
All Sizes	98%	81%	8%	9%	1%
1,000,000 or more	98%	72%	18%	7%	1%
500,000-999,999	99%	72%	13%	9%	5%
250,000-499,999	99%	84%	8%	4%	3%
100,000-249,999	98%	81%	13%	3%	2%
50,000-99,999	100%	76%	17%	6%	1%
25,000-49,999	99%	77%	10%	11%	1%
10,000-24,999	99%	82%	7%	9%	1%
2,500-9,999	99%	83%	7%	9%	—
Under 2,500	97%	82%	6%	9%	0

Source: U.S. Department of Justice (DOJ), Bureau of Justice Statistics. (2006). *Local Police Departments, 2003*. NCJ 210118. Washington, DC: U.S. Government Printing Office. p. 9.

Recruitment and Hiring

Once minimum hiring standards have been established, administrators can then move on to assessing their current practice of recruitment and hiring. Generally speaking, interest in law enforcement careers is waning, just as the daily duties of police officers continue to expand and diversify. This diminished interest in law enforcement as a career could be attributed to many reasons, but the average base minimum ($28,200) and maximum ($35,300) annual starting salaries may contribute *(DOJ, 2006, p. 11, Table 20)*. Even with these hurdles in place, it is essential to seek out quality candidates with varying personal characteristics and backgrounds to staff a successful department.

There was once a time when one police vacancy would attract a hundred interested candidates. This is no longer true. Additionally, the types of candidates who are applying often lack the diversity that an agency may be seeking. This diversity includes ethnicity, gender, sexual orientation and areas of college study. According to a 2003 Bureau of Justice Statistics survey, the percentage of male and female sworn personnel has been relatively stagnant in recent years. In 1987, women officers filled 7.6% of all full-time sworn police officers I. In 2003, 16 years later, that percentage had marginally increased to 11.3% *(2006, p. 7)*. A more recent survey conducted by the FBI reported the percentage of female full-time law enforcement personnel at 11.7% *(DOJ, 2008, Table 74)*. Regarding the race of full-time sworn personnel, 11.7% identify as Black/African American, 9.1% identify as Hispanic/Latino and 2.8% classify themselves as other *(DOJ, 2006, p. 7) (Table 8.2)*. This is surprising and disheartening considering the nation's emphasis on equality and affirmative action. Increasing the diversity of an agency will better support and meet the needs of the community that it serves. It is for these reasons that active and thoughtful recruitment be understood and emphasized by today's police administrators. Refer to chapter 6, Special Focus 6.2, regarding specific strategies to recruit diverse candidates.

Table 8.2: Bureau of Justice Table: Gender and race of full-time sworn personnel in local police departments, by size of population served, 2003

Population served	Male	Female	White	Black/African-American	Hispanic/Latino	Other
All Sizes	88.7%	11.3%	76.4%	11.7%	9.1%	2.8%
1,000,000 or more	82.7%	17.3%	61.1%	16.7%	19.3%	2.8%
500,000-999,999	84.4%	15.6%	61.9%	24.4%	7.8%	6.0%
250,000-499,999	85.4%	14.6%	66.6%	19.4%	11.3%	2.7%
100,000-249,999	89.0%	11.0%	76.0%	11.9%	9.1%	3.0%
50,000-99,999	91.2%	8.8%	83.3%	7.4%	7.0%	2.3%
25,000-49,999	91.8%	8.2%	87.5%	5.8%	5.5%	1.2%
10,000-24,999	93.3%	6.7%	90.4%	4.4%	3.0%	2.1%
2,500-9,999	93.8%	6.2%	89.8%	4.2%	3.4%	2.6%
Under 2,500	94.3%	5.7%	88.5%	5.7%	3.4%	2.5%

Source: U.S. Department of Justice (DOJ), Bureau of Justice Statistics. (2006). *Local Police Departments, 2003*. NCJ 210118. Washington, DC: U.S. Government Printing Office. p. 7.

Police Training

Once candidates are recruited and hired, they must be trained. From police recruits to veteran officers, all personnel need consistent and quality training. With the current economy and fiscal downturn, police administrators have been forced to trim spending. One area that has succumbed to this financial crisis is training. This has come at a critical time when citizen demands and expectations are expanding and new threats lurk on the horizon. Some agencies have cut non-essential training all together, while others have explored new training options.

One of the newest forms of police training is on-line programs. These are usually run by an established training agency or by the police department itself that has purchased the training software. Officers are provided with a user identification and are instructed to log on, read the training material and to then successfully pass an exam. This activity can usually be done while the officer is on regular duty and does not incur overtime expenses. The benefits to this type of training are the great reduction in costs, the consistency of the presentation, the well organized and structured material and the efficient use of an officer's uncommitted time.

There are two major disadvantages with online training. Having officers use their shift time to complete their training requirements takes them off of the street and away from their other duties. It should be noted, however, that the benefit of having officers drive around randomly in their patrol units has been questioned and research has shown that it has little value. On-duty training may be an effective use of officers' downtime. The other major disadvantage is that many people simply will not learn using this medium. As any education specialist would agree, there are different types of learners. Some people learn by doing, some by seeing, some by hearing and some by reading. Web-based training is limited in this capacity and will surely be retained by a lower number of students when compared to a more diverse instructional presentation.

Another training option is in-house classes conducted by employees. The advantages to this method are that it is less expensive, it makes use of uncommitted time, it can be tailored to meet the specific needs of each community and it provides staff with teaching opportunities. Allowing officers and supervisors to conduct training provides them with new challenges, improves their communication skills and hones their existing knowledge in the area that is presented.

There are also disadvantages to in-house training. Similar to web-based training, there may not always be time to fit in substantial training blocks and it does remove officers from the street if it is conducted on-duty. Also, some officers may not take the training seriously, as it is being conducted by a friend and/or coworker.

Police academies also offer training opportunities. Academies usually offer recruit training, specialized certification programs, annual certification classes and veteran officer review sessions. The advantages to academy training are that it is usually highly structured and universal and it may provide officers with a wanted change of pace in contrast to their daily tasks. However, this training may be expensive due to overtime costs and could be poor quality training, depending on the instructor.

Private businesses also offer a wide variety of police training. Well-known professionals, ranging from retired police officers to military personnel to practicing lawyers, conduct a diverse mix of training seminars nationwide. These training will usually include a greater variety of topics and opportunities. Also, they usually involve experienced professionals and practitioners who have a wealth of knowledge to offer to students. A final benefit to this type of training is that the curriculum is often fresh and includes up and coming technologies and new issues in the field. The major disadvantage of these privatized training is that they can be extremely expensive. Overtime costs, accommodations and class fees may make this option too cost-prohibitive for some administrators working with a thinning training budget.

Regardless of the training option that is used, the benefits of training should never be overlooked. One of the needs of the Millennial employee is to be challenged and exposed to new learning opportunities. To prevent boredom and to inspire creativity and new ideas, administrators need to support on-going training opportunities. This will ultimately improve morale, increase retention and improve police-community relations.

Personnel Evaluations

Another essential administrative responsibility is the establishment of and commitment to employee evaluations. Formal reviews are an essential component in any working environment that strives for employee development and professionalism. Ideally, evaluations consist of the formal review of each individual employee by direct supervisors who interact with and observe the officer on a consistent basis. Standardized evaluation procedures are used, as each officer is rated using the same system. Thorough evaluations should include a review of the employee's personal appearance, report writing, interactions with other employees and supervisors, officer safety, understanding of departmental policies and comprehension of criminal law and procedure. Evaluations should be conducted on a six-month or yearly basis. Supervisors should consult with each other to discuss the strengths and weaknesses of each employee. Activity data such as number of arrests and citations should be considered but attention to other activities such as problem solving, involvement in community activities, community relations and the submission of new ideas should also be included.

Formal evaluation periods are a great opportunity for officers to gather important feedback on their work and to guide them throughout their career. Rarely do officers sit down with supervisors and take the time to discuss their goals and interests. Review sessions provide this opportunity. Specific issues can be identified early on, before becoming a major problem. Strengths can be highlighted and encouraged. Evaluation sessions should involve open communication between the supervisor issuing the review and the officer. This should be considered a coaching session and a time to give positive and negative feedback in an appropriate environment.

The final portion of the written evaluation and the oral review is dedicated to the recommendation for future goals. Examples include:

"This employee should strive to engage in more self-initiated activity such as motor vehicle stops."

"This employee should seek out criminal investigations to begin to develop her investigative skills."

"This employee should seek out a specialized position as a Field Training Officer."

Using specific and articulate goals provides officers with direction and concrete tasks to work toward.

Outside of scheduled, formal reviews, employees also receive evaluation through informal feedback. This can come in the form of verbal praise or written emails from supervisors or other officers. While it may seem simple, it is rarely doled out by busy supervisors who may not grasp the importance of this type of feedback. Millennial employees in particular require an increased amount of positive feedback when compared to other generations. They enjoy a lot of praise and gentle coaching when errors are made.

In addition to formal reviews and informal coaching, another excellent program to draw attention to exemplary work is the formal commendation. Many agencies have ongoing or yearly awards that are given to individual officers for outstanding work. These are often issued to officers based on their involvement in particularly dangerous situations, where lives were saved or extreme courage was shown. While these actions certainly warrant commendation, other types of activities should also be recognized. Employees who start up and maintain new programs, who work tirelessly on major projects, who bring new ideas to the department, who show a long-term commitment to various programs or who show other exemplary actions, should also be considered for formal awards.

An important part of any formal awards program is to ensure that they are given out fairly and without prejudice. The best way to ensure that this occurs is to establish an awards committee that is diverse and that is comprised of a mix of employees from different ranks and different sections of the agency. All awards nominations should be considered and discussed. Any sort of favoritism shown by the awards committee will nullify the value of awards given and will contribute to poor morale.

New Technology

A final administrative function that can be easily disregarded is the constant updating of technology. As an employee, little is more frustrating than working with slow and inefficient technology that operates poorly and wastes time and energy. This can be a challenge to stay on top of, as technological advancements move at such a rapid pace. However, there are some straightforward programs and pieces of equipment that can easily improve employee satisfaction, efficiency and thoroughness. Computer software designed specifically for law enforcement is widely available and user-friendly. Hi-tech digital cameras and digital video recording devices are an amazing tool on any crime scene. In-cruiser cameras, interior surveillance cameras and remote operation cameras can provide useful information related to officer safety incidents, internal investigations, training points or criminal court trials. According to a 2003 survey, 60% of police departments regularly use video cameras and that can be broken down as follows: in patrol cars (55%), fixed-site surveillance (14%), traffic enforcement (11%) and mobile surveillance (8%) *(DOJ, 2006, p. 28).*

Technology is also important in the widely debated and scrutinized areas of police use of force and vehicle pursuits. Citizens expect that law enforcement agencies have a barrage of force options that will be effective and safe. Advances in technology have provided departments with rubber bullets, pepper ball guns, tasers and even web-throwers. If a situation occurs in which a less than lethal force option could have been used but was not available, it will likely create community-wide discontent. A 2003 survey indicated that 23% of police departments make use of infrared thermal imaging, 31% use tire deflation spikes and 7% use stolen vehicle tracking *(2006, p. 29) (Table 8.3).*

Many assume that the seemingly routine and logistical administrative functions of a police department are unrelated to effective policing strategies. However, the administration touches every member of a department and these fundamentals create a ripple effect throughout the agency. Administrators' actions and decisions have a critical role of setting the tone for the agency by planting the seeds for future success. Forward-thinking executives will have significant positive impacts on the overall atmosphere of a workplace. This environment contributes to pride and morale, and in turn, will make officers more trusting of administrative decisions, more open to change and more willing to explore new ideas and solutions.

Table 8.3: Bureau of Justice Chart: Types of nonlethal weapons authorized for personal use by sworn personnel in local police departments, by size of population served, 2003

Population served	Pepper Spray	Tear Gas	CS	Baton (any type)	Soft projectile	Electrical Device (stun/taser)	Rubber bullet
All Sizes	98%	16%	14%	95%	28%	23%	8%
1,000,000 or more	94%	19%	19%	100%	69%	75%	25%
500,000-999,999	97%	19%	22%	100%	48%	43%	16%
250,000-499,999	95%	24%	22%	100%	59%	56%	22%
100,000-249,999	99%	22%	24%	99%	66%	50%	22%
50,000-99,999	97%	25%	27%	99%	72%	46%	22%
25,000-49,999	100%	24%	21%	99%	57%	39%	19%
10,000-24,999	98%	22%	17%	97%	42%	31%	10%
2,500-9,999	98%	13%	14%	94%	28%	21%	6%
Under 2,500	98%	14%	12%	93%	13%	15%	6%

Source: U.S. Department of Justice (DOJ), Bureau of Justice Statistics. (2006). *Local Police Departments, 2003.* NCJ 210118. Washington, DC: U.S. Government Printing Office. p. 26.

End Notes

Commission on Accreditation for Law Enforcement Agencies (CALEA®), About CALEA®. Retrieved, September 3, 2009 from http://www.calea.org/Online/AboutCALEA/Commission.htm.

Commission on Accreditation for Law Enforcement Agencies (CALEA®). Law Enforcement Accreditation. Retrieved September 3, 2009 from http://www.calea.org/Online/CALEAPrograms/LawEnforcement/lawenfcost.htm.

J. Dixon, personal communication, September 28, 2009

Kasper, J. (2006, December). Proven Steps for Recruiting Women. *Law and Order*, 54(12), 63, 67.

Paynich, R. L. *The Impact of a College-Educated Police Force: A review of the literature* (Doctoral dissertation, Curry College, 2009).

U.S. Department of Justice (DOJ), Bureau of Justice Statistics. (2006, May). *Local police departments, 2003*. NCJ 210118. Washington, DC: U.S. Government Printing Office.

U.S. Department of Justice (DOJ), Bureau of Justice Statistics. (2007, June). *Census of State and Local Law Enforcement Agencies, 2004*. NCJ 212749. Washington, DC: U.S. Government Printing Office.

U.S. Department of Justice (DOJ), Federal Bureau of Investigation. (2008, September). *Crime in the United States, 2007*. Washington, DC: U.S. Government Printing Office.

Chapter 9
Police-Media Relations:
Actively Shaping the Public's
Image of the Police

M edia relations and its connection to the public image
may be an administrative function but it deserves
special attention. The union between the police and
the media has been turbulent over the years. From the coverage
of anti-war protests in the 1970s, to the repeated broadcast of
the Rodney King incident in 1993, the effects of the media on the
public's perception of the police and the resulting support of
the police has been well-illustrated. The direct link between the
media and police image cannot be successfully contested. A police
administrator who wants to foster a positive and accurate public
perception of a police department must work with the media and
not against it.

Defining Media

Before delving into the concept of media relations, it is
important to explore the nature of media. Many people may have
an established idea of what the media is but often are mistaken.
The Merriam-Webster Dictionary defines media as: "A medium
of cultivation, conveyance or expression" *(2009)*. It says nothing
about external agents or third parties that control news and
information. It is simply a means of communicating. This can
include television, newspaper, radio, the internet and many other
forms of communication.

Progressive administrators have recognized the potential
media opportunities that the police can take control of in an effort
to improve and maintain a positive public image. Police
departments do not have to be the victims of the media. Law
enforcement in the new century requires that police officers
proactively seek and establish reliable relationships with media
members and produce their own communication mediums. They
cannot sit back and allow the media to create a negative or

inaccurate image and must instead work to shape it into a well-balanced and representative reflection of the agency.

Developing Positive Working Relationships with the Members of the Media

One way to improve media coverage is to establish healthy working relationships with representatives from various media outlets. Identify one or two members of a department who will be media liaisons and encourage them to reach out to specific individuals who work consistently on crime reporting or police news. All media outlets should be welcomed, including local newspapers, television stations, radio stations and high school or college campus news organizations. When news does occur, have the same individuals engage in communication with the media outlets. This will inspire trust and should work to build stronger relationships between all parties.

In addition to having media liaisons, members of the media should be invited to police events. Ribbon-cutting ceremonies, awards dinners, specialized training and community outreach and education programs are all great examples of events that should have a media presence. These events are extremely valuable to members of the media and their viewers who will see a more equal balance of news stories involving the police *(Special Focus 9.1)*.

Self-promotion

It may seem like an insurmountable challenge to develop a positive public image through media as the police-media relationship has historically been strained. However, with the fast-paced developments in new technologies, self-promotion and marketing has never been easier. The following strategies highlight some of the techniques that can be used to work toward a positive police image by empowering police departments to produce their own news and information reporting systems.

Special Focus 9.1: Generating Positive Media Coverage: The 2008 and 2009 Citizen Police Academies Held by the Northampton, Massachusetts Police Department

The Northampton Police Department held its first Citizen Police Academy (CPA) in the mid 1990s. Although it was an incredibly successful program, collective bargaining issues resulted in the loss of the program. In the winter of 2008 the department restarted the program and conducted its first Citizen Police Academy (CPA) in over a decade. The academy was held one night a week for ten weeks. James F. Lowe, a local newspaper reporter who was assigned to cover police activity in the region, applied for the program. He was an active participant who engaged in class discussions as well as hands-on activities. Once he completed the course he wrote an article that appeared in the March 29, 2008 copy of the *Daily Hampshire Gazette* titled, "Blue Surge—19 citizens. 1 police department. Many lessons." The article appeared on the front page of the paper and generated a lot of interest in the program. The following year the number of applicants exceeded the available spaces.

In the winter of 2009, Northampton Police conducted a second academy. This time Kathy Reynolds, a reporter with a local television news station, and Alan Rosko, a videographer with the same news agency, applied and were granted access to the program. They were active participants through the course and became friendly with many of the instructors. They interviewed other class participants and took video footage from all of the classes. They then created and produced weekly news segments as part of their evening broadcasts. These were well received by community members who continually approached officers on the street saying, "I saw you on the news last night!"

The collaboration between the media and the police in both of these programs benefited all who were involved directly and the many readers and viewers who had the opportunity to see their police department from a new perspective.

Reprinted with permission from Captain Joseph Koncas, Northampton, MA PD.

Police Website

A critical tool of every police agency is the creation and maintenance of a website. Websites serve a multitude of purposes. They are a reliable resource for community members who have questions about a myriad of police issues, including: sex offenders, obtaining police reports, understanding firearms laws, emergency and non-emergency contact information and departmental emails, general crime data and statistics and many other topics. Having informational, accurate and updated information on a department's website can reduce the workload of administrative assistants, dispatchers and police who spend valuable time answering these simple questions.

In addition to providing the average citizen with useful information, websites should also be considered primary recruiting tools. Most applicants that are considering employment with an agency will visit their website. In addition to seeking basic employment information such as minimum requirements and testing dates, they will be assessing the department's professionalism, opportunities for specialization, uniform and cruiser appearance and activity levels. They will also be viewing images of officers to ascertain what kind of department it is and whether or not they believe they will fit in. Recall from chapter eight the importance of highlighting diversity in images of department members in recruiting materials. This includes images on websites and departments should aim to use images that are reflective of the types of candidates that they seek to hire.

In addition to simple and clear contact information, websites should always include an area for community feedback. Both positive and negative feedback should be welcomed as administrators should look for opportunities for improvement. It is important that community members feel heard and that their opinions and ideas are respected and considered. Administrators should review feedback and be sure to respond to those individuals who took the time to communicate with their police department.

"Ask a Cop" Programs

Another interesting community policing concept in the area of media relations is the "Ask a Cop" or "Ask the Chief" programs. Some brave police chiefs and officers have taken on the role of answering community questions during radio shows or local cable access programs. This can be an excellent means of opening communication between the people and their police. For those that may experience stage fright under the pressure of live questioning, an alternative is to maintain a weekly column in the newspaper that invites questions each week that are answered by members of the police department. Both of these strategies are illustrative of proactive strategies that will reduce barriers between the people and the police by opening lines of communication.

Public Service Announcements

Police agencies can also seek to create public service announcements that are designed for radio or television. Police officers can use these to broadcast safety tips, remind citizens of the enforcement of specific laws such as drunk driving or lack of seatbelt use or introduce changes in laws that will have a direct impact on citizens.

Creating Media Materials

A final way to improve police-community relations through the media is to produce informational handouts, mailers or yearly summaries that are available to all citizens. This is common practice in the United Kingdom, where many police agencies create a yearly summary of activities including crime statistics, new technologies, investigative clearance rates, personal accomplishments and future goals of the agency. These summaries will not be free to produce and distribute but their contribution to the image of the police in a given community may be invaluable.

Contributions to the Police Image

When considering an agency's public image, one must recognize how that image is created. While some people have experienced individual contacts with police officers performing their duties, many others have never had a substantial interaction with a police officer, outside of receiving a traffic citation. Knowing this, one must ask, how does the public's perception of its police department form? The answer to that question will include the media.

Police administrators who recognize this link are encouraged to take control. Establish and maintain positive media contacts and produce internal media material. The people's perception of their police department will determine whether or not they trust the police, whether they engage in open communication with the police, whether they engage in community education programs, whether they collaborate with the police to solve problems and whether or not they will support financial expenditures for police departments such as new technologies, new vehicles or enhanced staffing.

End Notes

Media [2]. (2009). In Merriam-Webster Online Dictionary. Retrieved October 6, 2009, from http://www.merriam-webster. com/dictionary/media[2]

The most visible members of any police department are the patrol officers. When people think of the police, they often envision a uniformed officer in a cruiser. Patrol officers comprise the majority of personnel and are tasked with an ever-expanding list of duties. They handle the most calls and as a result have the most interactions with the public. This is often through motor vehicle law enforcement. One survey revealed that of all the people who reported contact with the police in 2005, 56.3% indicated that their contact was traffic-related *(DOJ, 2007, p. 3, Table 3)*. These individuals had either been the operator or passenger during a traffic stop or had been involved in a traffic collision. It is for this reason that effective policing maintains a heavy focus on patrol officers and their problem-solving techniques and interactions with the public. Integrating positive community contacts into everyday operations is an essential component of the police-citizen relationship that is necessary in order for a present day police agency to develop and maintain support internal and external support.

Key Components of Effective Patrol Methods

Although we have moved beyond the Community Policing Era, there are *four essential components* of that philosophy related specifically to patrol officers that should be carried over into the new era by contemporary police supervisors.

Proactive Approach

The first of these effective methods is the focus on proactive strategies. This requires that the rank and file identify issues and apply the problem solving process to these issues in order to prevent them from recurring. This strategy can be used to respond to community problems such as persistent graffiti, motor vehicle breaks, thefts, litter, motor vehicle infractions, noise complaints and drug and alcohol activity. The philosophy of community policing supports Goldstein's SARA method. This requires that departments scan the situation to identify the problem, analyze it to determine why it is ongoing, respond with preventative methods and then assess the situation after a preventative technique has been applied to determine if it was successful. This is at the heart of all proactive patrol strategies *(Special Focus 10.1)*.

Special Focus 10.1: Sheriff's Theft Offense Prosecution Program (STOPP), Fairfield County, Ohio, Sheriff's Office

Members of the Fairfield County Sheriff's Office recognized that their community was experiencing a rash of motor vehicle breaks. During an interview with Sgt. Alex Lape, he indicated that theft from motor vehicles was their "number one problem in populated areas." The items that were stolen included GPS systems, cell phones, iPods, laptop computers and almost anything of value inside vehicles. The items were then being pawned at local shops or sold on the street. To combat this problem, Sgt. Lape created the Sheriff's Theft Offense Prosecution Program (STOPP). The program involved a combination of strategies to identify suspects and to reduce this type of crime:

- Review of reported past incidents to determine time of day and day of week that most thefts occurred.

- The use of plainclothes and uniformed officers saturating targeted areas during targeted times. This included foot and vehicle surveillance.

- Effective communication with pawn shops and review of pawn records that could be compared to stolen item lists.

- The use of computer software that is directly linked to local pawn shops that officers can access to review sell sheets.

Using this multi-angled approach, the first operational wave was conducted on July 18, 2009. The program was incredibly successful. For two and a half weeks after the first operation, they did not receive a single report of thefts from motor vehicles. Additionally, several suspects were identified and were charged with varying offenses. Sgt. Lape indicated that the program was "almost too successful" because they developed so many leads from community contacts, pawn shop employees and other sources, they have not had the time to follow up on all of them. This program is an excellent example of the SARA method put into practice and a creative and detailed solution to a community's crime problem.

Reprinted with permission of Sgt. Alex Lape, Fairfield County Sheriff's Office

Geographic Patrol Assignment

A second major component of community policing that should be retained by today's police administrators is the use of geographic patrol assignment. Prior to the growth of community policing, administrators who understood the importance of beat familiarity and community connections wisely assigned each officer to the same patrol area each shift. This allowed officers to familiarize themselves with the people in specific neighborhoods, the businesses, the vehicle traffic and the physical layout of their areas. Many officers also developed a sense of pride and personal accountability for the activities of their beat areas. With the move into the Community Policing Era, geographic patrol assignment was formally recognized for its many benefits and its link to successful community policing strategies. As of 2003, it was reported that 31% of agencies used geographic assignments for patrol officers *(DOJ, 2006, p. 21, Table 45)*. For larger departments (serving over 50,000 residents) this patrol strategy was much more common with an average of 86% using this method *(p. 21, Table 45)*. It is logical that larger departments would use this strategy, as smaller departments may have a single officer covering an entire town and geographic assignments would not be applicable.

Accountability

Accountability was first recognized as an essential element of a department during the Reform Era. It was highlighted throughout the Community Policing Era and should be maintained as agencies move forward. Individual accountability is reflected in the geographic patrol assignments but departmental accountability extends to supervisors and executives alike. To be accountable, administrators must make deployment decisions based on fact and reason. It wouldn't make sense to assign all officers on a department to bike patrol, just as it wouldn't make sense to have all available officers patrol one area of a city while another is left unattended. Patrol assignments must be made thoughtfully and must be adaptable to change. The best deployment strategies will ensure that the most effective patrol methods (vehicle, foot, bike, etc.) are employed in the right areas at the right time so that community members will best be served. Administrators should base their decisions on community concerns, population distribution and the crime rate in specific areas. All decisions should be data-driven so that, if challenged, executives can easily explain patrol methods and deployment strategies.

Community Partnerships and Collaboration

The fourth and final community policing element strongly connected to the uniformed patrol force is the creation of community partnerships through collaboration. Officers must have the ability to recognize problems and have the communication skills and contacts to reach out to citizens in order to best handle the issues. If an officer continually responds to motor vehicle accidents on a specific section of roadway, the best strategy would utilize community contacts with neighbors, local businesses and the city department of public works. This collaboration of citizens and city employees could generate unique ideas to slow traffic including enhancing street lighting, increasing speeding enforcement or reducing speed limits. In this scenario, participants should feel valued and empowered by their own ability to work together to problem-solve and by seeing their ideas put into action *(Special Focus 10.2)*.

Special Focus 10.2: Hampshire County Sexual Assault Response Team (SART)

Rebecca Lockwood is the Associate Director of the Everywoman's Center at the University of Massachusetts in Amherst. The Center is a resource for women who are dealing with a variety of issues, including sexual assault. In 2009, Lockwood recognized that uniting the resources that currently serve survivors of sexual assault, could benefit everyone involved. With that in mind, Lockwood created a Sexual Assault Response Team (SART) to serve the Hampshire County area. The area is somewhat unique in that there are five major colleges and universities within the county. The Hampshire County SART members are made up of a prosecutor from the District Attorney's office, emergency room nurses who treat sexual assault victims and administer sexual assault evidence collection kits, hospital administrators, victim/witness advocates and campus and municipal police officers and administrators. During the first meeting the team identified specific hurdles that they face when assisting survivors of sexual assault. Some of the concerns that were brought up included:

- Some victims reported to counselors that they were nervous to speak with the police about the incident because they were unsure if they wanted to have charges filed.

- In the evening campus health centers close and survivors often lack adequate transportation to local hospitals.

- Dispatchers are a critical link in the process of reporting sexual assaults and for gathering important information that they may have to testify to in court. It was unclear whether or not they had training specific to handling sexual assault calls.

- Campus police officers sometimes made errors in their investigations. It was believed that these errors were caused by lack of experience and a high turnover rate.

Additionally, municipal police officers received annual in-service training on this subject, while it was unclear whether or not campus police received this same training.

- Establishing "best practices" for response effort.

- Maintaining consistency in response efforts.

In response to these identified needs, the SART team discussed ideas to address each issue. The solutions included the following:

- Created a training program designed for campus police officers regarding sexual assault investigation and present the curriculum to all of the local campus police officers.

- Local police departments enhanced their websites by adding informational pages that were designed for survivors of sexual assaults who were seeking information.

- To alleviate the transportation issue, the five colleges collaborated to have one on-call driver available after hours to drive sexual assault survivors to the local hospital.

- Dispatch centers were contacted and were offered free training on taking calls from sexual assault survivors.

The SART team continues to operate in Hampshire County and meets on a monthly basis. New ideas are brought forward and any complications from recent cases are brought up and addressed. The team continues to work for improved sexual assault response on behalf of all agencies involved.

The SART is an excellent example of community colla-boration at its best. Police officers and representatives from other agencies work together to identify problems and find solutions.

Reprinted with permission of Rebecca Lockwood, Assoc. Dir. of Everywoman's Center

Forms of Patrol

It is clear that effective policing is directly linked to patrol operations and its success requires officer participation. The next step is to identify and assess historic and current patrol methods. Administrators have become quite creative in this area, as officers nationwide can be seen patrolling on a variety of modes of transportation, including rollerblades and Segways. Although these methods may be effective, there are more traditional non-vehicle options that have become more mainstream over the past few decades. A 2003 survey of routine patrol methods revealed that 59% of departments regularly use foot patrol, 38% use bicycles, 14% use motorcycles, 4% use boats and 2% use horses *(DOJ, 2006, page 13, Table 24)*. With this wide variety of methods, each type has identifiable advantages and disadvantages.

Cruiser Patrol

The most widely used and widely recognized patrol method is the car. Police departments have a long history of using cruisers as their primary patrol methods. They have been trusted for their ability to rapidly respond to calls, transport equipment and people, cover a large geographic area and for their visible presence. A marked vehicle has an impact on citizen behavior, as merely parking an empty cruiser on an interstate is an effective means of slowing traffic. Cruisers are certainly the most practical and, for the time being, a necessary component of a police agency. They do have their disadvantages however. Vehicles are expensive to buy, outfit and to operate. They consume fuel and have a negative environmental impact associated with fuel consumption and the resulting exhaust. Outside of cost and pollution, vehicles separate the people from the police. Officers driving through a neighborhood with their windows up, air conditioning on and radio playing will do little to create and maintain positive community contacts.

Bicycle Patrol

A second common patrol method is the bicycle. It is a common misconception that the use of bike patrol officers is indicative of an agency that has adopted community policing. However, utilizing bicycle officers is a patrol method and has no relation to a department's philosophy. Due to its many advantages, bike patrol officers are incredibly common. One major advantage is the low cost associated with a bicycle patrol unit. When compared to vehicles, the costs associated with the training, equipment, uniforms and routine maintenance are substantially less. Another significant advantage is the improved health of officers who are riding bicycles each day instead of spending an eight hour shift sitting in a cramped patrol car wearing a 20 pound duty belt. Bike officers can also have faster response times than cruisers or foot officers in certain regions. This is especially true in congested areas or places that are not accessible to vehicle traffic. Bike officers are also highly visible and more approachable. Citizens may feel more comfortable walking up to a bike officer and simply have more opportunity to do so than if the officer was in a cruiser. However, bike units do have some disadvantages. The officers cannot carry much equipment, cannot transport prisoners and do not generally operate in cold or wet weather.

Foot Patrol

Walking a beat is the oldest form of police patrol. Before the advent of vehicles and other alternative modes of transportation, those tasked with protecting communities were resigned to walking. Similar to bike patrol officers, those walking the beat are approachable and are likely to have interactions with people on the street. Business owners often give friendly nods, curious children ask officers about their gear and passersby may ask the officer for directions or restaurant recommendations. These contacts may seem trivial but they are incredibly important pieces of building partnerships and facilitating communication. Walking is also useful in that it can be used inside and outside. Officers who are walking the beat are more likely to walk into stores, other buildings or through parks that would not normally have a police presence. Finally, assigning officers to walk is another way to maintain or improve officer health. Of course foot officers cannot carry large equipment and cannot respond to calls quickly. They are reliant on the assistance of officers in cruisers who can carry medical supplies, paperwork, safety equipment and who can transport prisoners. Foot officers are also more limited in the area that they can cover and will have dramatically smaller beats when compared to officers in cars or on bike.

Park and Walk Programs

Many departments, whose resources may be limited but who still understand the value of these assorted patrol methods, have successfully implemented park and walk programs. These programs require that officers who are assigned a patrol car for their eight hour shift park the cruiser for a specified amount of time and get out and walk around predetermined target areas. These target areas may include downtown business districts, schools, parks, high-crime areas, close-quarter residential areas or any other location that would benefit from this type of program. The officers are required to walk for a set amount of time, such as two hours during an eight hour shift. The benefits to this program include fuel savings, improved officer health, increased visibility and presence in formally unpatrolled areas, enhanced community contacts and the development of officer familiarity with locations that are not normally accessed. Of particular note is the development of knowledge related to the interior of schools. With a national focus on school safety and security, a department's ability to best respond to school incidents is a necessity. A key element of successful response is knowledge of the layout of the building including entrances and exits and stairwells. If there is an active shooter situation, officers will rarely have time to review blueprints before entering. Park and walk programs are an ideal familiarization strategy that can be used for this purpose.

In order for this program to work, the planning team must first review their city or town and identify areas that would benefit from walk-throughs. Area officers will be informed of the specific locations within their areas that should be checked and officers will be required to notify dispatch of their walk-throughs so that they can be monitored. This information will not only be useful for supervisors who want to be aware of their officers' activities, but it will also be useful to police administrators who may be challenged to answer questions about patrol strategies and methods. The exact number of hours that officers park their cruisers and walk target areas will be documented and will be available for public inquiry.

Park and walk programs are easy to implement. A few short planning sessions and the creation of a directive will be the only time required to begin. It can be used in small towns and big cities. It is a program that is catching on across the United States, as police executives do their best to balance high visibility and positive community contacts with personnel shortages and tightened budgets. This is a great way to make use of an officer's uncommitted time that might normally be spent chatting on a cell phone, reading or parked on the side of the road monitoring traffic.

The ideal strategy for a police administrator is to use a combination of various patrol methods. Each has its own strengths and weaknesses, but the increase in one-on-one contacts using non-vehicle methods cannot be overlooked. It is for this reason that alternative methods are so strongly associated with fostering citizen contacts and improving a department's image. Any agency that wants to increase positive community contacts and build these partnerships will work to intertwine all the various patrol methods.

End Notes

U.S. Department of Justice (DOJ), Bureau of Justice Statistics. (2007, April). *Contacts Between Police and the Public, 2005.* NCJ 215243. Washington, DC: U.S. Government Printing Office.

U.S. Department of Justice (DOJ), Bureau of Justice Statistics. (2006, May). *Local police departments, 2003.* NCJ 210118. Washington, DC: U.S. Government Printing Office.

Chapter 11
Community Outreach:
Proven Strategies That Work

A t the heart of every successful police department are thoughtfully considered community outreach and education programs. These programs encourage citizen-police collaboration and communication. They are an excellent opportunity to incorporate positive contact with the public into everyday services. They provide officers with new challenges and allow them to expand their duties to include tasks that may contribute to improved morale and job satisfaction. With their many proven benefits, they are an essential component of any progressive police organization.

Similar to the expansion of patrol methods, there are a plethora of programs that have been created and implemented over the past few decades. Programs may involve police officers playing basketball with kids, working alongside elders, hosting camps for children, teaching safety classes and a myriad of others. While all of these programs may have been developed to address specific issues in a certain community, there are several strategies that are more popular and can be almost universally applied to agencies across the United States, and the world. This chapter will identify distinct programs that have been successfully implemented at police departments nationwide.

Citizen Police Academy

One of the best community policing programs functioning today is the Citizen Police Academy (CPA). The first such program was created and implemented in the United Kingdom in 1977. It was incredibly well received and the concept quickly spread. The Orlando, Florida Police Department is credited with operating the first citizen academy in the United States in 1985 (http://www.nationalcpaa.org/faq.htm). Again, the program was a huge success and citizen academies have been implemented in police departments nationwide. A Bureau of Justice survey indicated that 17% of police agencies conducted citizen police academies in 2003 *(DOJ, 2006, p. 21, Table 46)*.

A citizen police academy is a "police school" for members of a community who want to learn more about their individual police department and law enforcement in general. The program is organized and instructed by police officers and administrators. The curriculum usually includes an assortment of topics such as use of force, forensics, sexual assault investigations, narcotics, gangs, patrol procedures, motor vehicle law, accident investigation, domestic violence, search and seizure and firearms. In most cases a mix of classroom lectures, demonstrations, hands-on activities and local case examples related to each topic have proven to be an engaging and effective curriculum portfolio.

The benefits of conducting a CPA extend beyond the obvious. It is true that citizens will learn more about police operations and personnel and consequently, may be more sympathetic and objective when they see news stories in the media. Additionally, these academies illustrate openness and facilitate communication between the police and the people. Beyond these advantages are the many benefits to those who organize and instruct a class for the CPA. It is a perfect fit for the Millennial employee who is seeking new opportunities and challenges. It will instill a sense of pride and increased morale among participating staff within an agency. While so many officers continually engage in negative interactions and conflict while working the street, the citizen academy is a place where officers can have positive citizen contacts *(Special Focus 11.1)*. It is also a rare opportunity for officers to engage with members of the community that they may not otherwise encounter.

Special Focus 11.1: Improving the Police Image: Anonymous Surveys Collected from Participants of a 2009 Citizen Police Academy

"I have greatly enjoyed this program to the point that I have talked about this program to friends, family and neighbors."

"The perspective I gained is what I liked most about this program. I learned that police officers are very human, friendly, have good sense of humor."

"This is the best PR you could have—I recommend it to be run as often as possible."

"This course was very informative and increased my understanding of NPD. It is a great community education tool since I now can evaluate newspaper stories or complaints about police because I have a better understanding of police procedure and laws and actual human beings who are police officers."

"The entire department was fantastic. I loved getting to know them. I can't say enough about how accessible and friendly everyone was. Great class!"

"I was impressed with the professionalism of all the members of the police department. This is an excellent program for giving insight into what your jobs entail. I am leaving with a greater appreciation and admiration for the fine job the whole force is doing. I have discussed these classes for the last ten weeks with my friends, family and acquaintances. There are a lot of people who are interested in participating in future programs."

"My respect for NPD went up immensely from having taken the course."

"I always had the assumption that a lot of people became cops for the power. These past weeks have really shown me that there are police that are truly doing what they're doing to help, to improve the community they live and work in."

Reprinted with permission of Captain Joseph Koncas, Northampton, MA PD.

Ride-along Programs

Ride-along programs are also a great way for citizens to better learn about their police department and to develop a personal connection with an individual officer. It is also another way that officers can have positive contacts with the people that they serve. These programs involve a citizen riding with a host officer for all or part of their shift. An agency may choose to incorporate this program into the citizen police academy by encouraging graduates of the CPA to participate in a ride-along. This culminating event after graduation is a prime opportunity for participants to see everything that they learned put into practice.

Strict guidelines need to be written so that the officer and citizen fully understand the conditions of the ride-along. For example, host officers with a citizen in the cruiser with them should not engage in vehicle pursuits. Also, citizens cannot be brought onto crime scenes where they could inadvertently contaminate the area. They cannot be allowed to see certain controlled information, such as criminal histories or the identity of particular crime victims. Departments that are interested in this program must also have a waiver that excuses the city or town from being held liable if the person is injured. All of these restrictions are fairly simple to implement. A ride-along program is easy to manage and is a great opportunity for curious citizens, local politicians, and those that are interested in a career in law enforcement or members of the media to see the daily activities of a police officer.

Park and Walk

Another successful community program is the Park and Walk. This concept was covered in Chapter 10, but it is a worthwhile hybrid of a patrol method and a community outreach program that deserves consideration in this chapter as well. The biggest benefits are the increases in the number of positive community contacts and approachability of officers walking a beat.

Neighborhood Watch

Neighborhood Watch programs are another example of a successful police-community program *(Special Focus 11.2)*. This usually consists of a group of citizens who may collaborate with a police liaison. They often meet once a week or once a month to discuss neighborhood issues and to brainstorm to pinpoint solutions. Examples might include graffiti, abandoned property, such as homes, businesses or vehicles, litter, theft or loud parties. They often erect street signs or stickers on homes that indicate participation in the program. Neighbors look out for each other and accept some accountability for the neighborhoods in which they live. This is a great way for citizens to feel connected to each other and to their police department and may instill a sense of community that had previously not existed.

Special Focus 11.2: Neighborhood Watch, Farmington Hills, Michigan Police Department

The Farmington Hills Police Department maintains a number of excellent community outreach programs. One such program, Neighborhood Watch, has been a successful part of their department for over 20 years.

In Farmington Hills, any subdivision or block may initiate a Neighborhood Watch as long as 50% or more of the residents agree to participate. Once a majority of citizens in a designated area elect to take part in this program they select an individual to work as the subdivision or block coordinator. This individual acts as the primary liaison between the community and the police department. The coordinator can then contact the department's Crime Prevention Section and a police officer will be assigned to their neighborhood.

Citizen participants must attend a Neighborhood Watch Orientation meeting that provides individuals with knowledge regarding the organization, rules, criminal law and the capabilities of the police department. For citizens that cannot attend the meeting, the department has an informational video that can be viewed instead. In these meetings, residents learn that the goal of a Neighborhood Watch program is to encourage neighbors to look out for each other and for participants to act as "an extra set of eyes" for the police department. Individuals learn what type of information officers will need if they respond to a report of suspicious activity in the area. Residents are also reminded not engage with suspicious characters. "The program is intended to make citizens more vigilant, not turn them into vigilantes."

Once residents have attended their informational meeting, they receive decals and Neighborhood Watch pamphlets that contain instructions on:

- Reporting suspicious behavior

- General home security

- Lock and security device options

Once the start-up activities have been completed the coordinators are expected to schedule regular community meetings. Meetings are held to discuss neighborhood concerns, to encourage the community concept and to strengthen personal relationships. Additionally, the Crime Prevention Officer assigned to the area may attend these meetings to provide residents with information and updates or to hear concerns and answer questions. The Farmington Hills Police also distribute bi-monthly newsletters to Neighborhood Watch coordinators in an effort to further share information.

In addition to Neighborhood Watch, the Farmington Hills Police also offer a Business Watch. This program mirrors the residential program but instead involves business owners and employees. Information provided to participants includes crimes and schemes that specifically target businesses.

Both of these programs are excellent examples of successfully outreach programs that are designed to address quality of life issues, prevent crime and encourage citizen involvement.

Reprinted with permission of Chief Charles Nebus, Farmington Hills, MI PD.

Self-defense Programs

Many police agencies offer Rape Aggression Defense (RAD) classes or other personal safety programs. These have become a staple for many campus police departments that allow students to participate and receive course credit for their completion. Self-defense classes may include the fairly rigid RAD training or may involve other classes on general safety and decision-making. These courses are a valuable opportunity for police officers to interact positively with community members and to participate in new and challenging tasks.

Police Week/Police Day

Many police agencies host a Police Week or a Police Day. This is similar to an open house that a school might offer, where citizens are invited to come to the police station to meet officers, get tours of the facilities, see the inside of the cruisers and participate in hands-on activities. These may include running a radar or lidar gun, lifting fingerprints or trying on body armor. As part of this event, agencies may include bicycle registration, Child ID kits or gun-lock giveaways. Organizers may also incorporate a 5k run or a bike race to emphasize fitness and fun. They may also serve as fund-raisers for police-related causes. Some cities host Public Safety day where fire departments, ambulance services and police all unite. The benefits of such events include open communication with the public, positive police-community contacts and the pride that employees may feel while "showing off" their respective agencies.

Interns

Another fantastic program that departments should explore is the use of interns. Colleges and universities are often seeking placement locations for students studying criminal justice. These internships offer a great opportunity for students to explore the field of policing, volunteer their time and contribute to the daily operations of a police department. Interns are usually limited to administrative duties in the station. They can engage in data entry, filing, answering phones or a myriad of other duties that would be appropriate. Allowing interns to work alongside officers builds community relations, may increase the number of interested applicants when vacancies arise and can improve officer morale as they see new faces excited and interested in the duties of a police officer.

Other Outreach Activities

In truth, there are almost endless possibilities when it comes to community outreach and education programs. Some officers may engage in lectures, conduct training, staff departmental booths at fairs, speak at career days or organize sports teams. There is a healthy variety when it comes to community programs and the diversity within staff at a police agency is adeptly able to meet the needs of all of these programs.

Citizen Surveys

The citizen survey is beyond the realm of a specific program but still within the genre of community outreach. Citizen surveys are an excellent way to gather different types of information from the public. Surveys might focus on satisfaction with police services in general, perceptions of crime problems/fear of crime, police-community contacts, program evaluation, personal crime experiences or a mix of these topics. As of 1997, 30% of departments reported using some form of a citizen survey *(DOJ, 2001, p. 7, Table 11)*. As of 1999, that number dropped to 28% *(page 7, Table 11)* and as of 2003 that number plunged to 22% *(DOJ, 2006, p. 22, Table 47)*. Although the use of citizen surveys seems to be diminishing, their value should cause progressive administrators to reconsider implementing some form of a survey method to gather invaluable data.

The financial cost associated with the production, mailing and processing of citizen surveys may be prohibitive but there are other options. Some administrators have collaborated with other city departments to have the surveys included in other mailings such as real estate or excise tax bills. Other strategies include the use of phone surveys, email surveys linked with the departmental website or making surveys available at large events such as fairs or other community events.

The information obtained from surveys can be useful in many ways. A 2003 study revealed that departments use survey results in the following ways (2006, p. 22):

- Evaluate an agency's performance (76%)

- Provide information to patrol officers (61%)

- Evaluate officer performance (49%)

- Evaluate program effectiveness (45%)

- Prioritize crime and disorder problems (43%),

- Allocation of resources to neighborhoods (38%)

- Training curriculum development (37%)

In addition to providing police personnel with valuable information that may impact resource deployment and training, surveys are also useful to build community relationships. Citizens feel empowered and are appreciative that their police department is asking for their feedback and suggestions. This technique can open the avenues of communication and may work to reduce the "us versus them" barrier.

The many benefits of community outreach and education programs far exceed the most obvious impact of citizen education. Participants do develop a better understanding of police operations and may be less likely to make quick judgments when the department is under fire. In addition, these programs also build positive personal contacts, thereby reducing the barrier that can exist between a police officer and a citizen. Officers will have more opportunities to think creatively and to use different skills. They may re-spark an officer's interest who had been idling in a certain position. Reaching out to individuals and groups will contribute to an overall improved public image of an agency and illustrates a proactive and progressive response to community issues. All of these benefits contribute to an individual employee's personal sense of pride and respect and this is essential for today's Millennial employees.

The ideas for community outreach and education programs are almost limitless. Departments nationwide have implemented creative and effective programs that have been well-received and reproduced in other communities. Each city or town will have its own unique needs and issues that will need to be individually assessed to determine the best action. The programs mentioned in this chapter have a strong track record of success. The world of law enforcement has moved beyond the traditional police methods of random patrol and rapid response. Limiting an agency to these techniques is short-sighted. Today's police administrators should strive to integrate proactive and successful community outreach and education strategies with everyday operations.

End Notes

Citizen Police Academy (http://www.nationalcpaa.org/faq.htm)

U.S. Department of Justice (DOJ), Bureau of Justice Statistics. (2001, February). *Community Policing in Local Police Departments, 1997 and 1999.* NCJ 184794. Washington, DC: U.S. Government Printing Office.

U.S. Department of Justice (DOJ), Bureau of Justice Statistics. (2006, May). *Local police departments, 2003.* NCJ 210118. Washington, DC: U.S. Government Printing Office.

Prior to April 20, 1999, there had been only nominal attention paid to school safety and security beyond the scope of fire drills and breaking up schoolyard fights. School was generally considered a safe place and the majority of parents and students had little concern about life-threatening incidents occurring on school grounds. All of that changed when Eric Harris and Dylan Klebold went on a shooting rampage through Columbine High School in Colorado, killing 12 people, injuring 24 and then killing themselves. The incident commanded immediate national attention as the vulnerability of teachers, staff and students in America's schools became apparent.

The Columbine incident brought to light many different areas of concern regarding school safety. Early scrutiny of the event revolved around how two teenage boys had gained access to such an assortment of guns and ammunition. But as the days and months passed, new concerns emerged regarding bullying, building access, agency interoperability, critical incident planning and first responder preparedness.

The recognition of these many issues forced police and school administrators to re-evaluate crisis preparedness. The necessity of a strong school-police alliance extending to all levels of public and private education became apparent. While it is still incredibly safe to be at school, concern for active shooters, bombs or threats of terrorists attacking these "soft targets" has motivated many police agencies to work diligently toward both prevention and effective response.

Over the past few decades there have been a variety of methods that have been implemented in response to issues regarding school safety. The best overall method is to employ an integrated strategy that involves both proactive and reactive planning. This chapter highlights strategies that have proven to be effective in communities across the nation.

Communication and Collaboration: The School-Police Connection

As with so many of the programs covered thus far, effective school-based strategies begin with solid communication and collaboration. A police department, regardless of size, should have a school liaison officer who is the direct contact person for school administrators. The liaison should work with school personnel by attending monthly meetings to discuss specific issues related to school safety and security.

An effective starting point in the creation of a police-school alliance is to create a Memorandum of Understanding (MOU) between the two agencies so that the needs of both can best be met. Debating the right decision and jockeying for power has no place in the midst of a crisis and preplanning for how two agencies will work together effectively is a necessity. These written agreements may include a section that targets early identification of problems. All too often problem activities at school are known only to the school and problem activities on the street are known only to the police. A method of sharing information between the two agencies can be helpful to all involved. For example, if two juveniles are arrested for fighting with each other on a weekend, this behavior is likely to carry over to the school environment. Notifying school administrators of this type of event may prevent further issues from occurring or escalating within the school.

Once the MOU has been written, the major goals of the group are to share information through effective communication and to plan for critical incidents. This planning process is a long one and should involve multiple representatives from each department that will extend beyond the scope of the single police liaison and school administrators. Strategies for handling crises require representatives from all emergency response agencies, including local police, fire, medical services, state police, dispatchers, public works employees, city political figures, parents and others. The ultimate goal is to create a detailed response plan for specific incidents. This plan should be re-evaluated and adjusted as buildings are modified, security systems are upgraded, personnel change and other events occur that may impact the implementation of the plan. It is imperative that these plans be consistently assessed and tested for effectiveness.

Incident Training and Drills: Preparing for the Worst

Once the school-police union has been formed and critical response plans have been formulated, it is the responsibility of all involved departments to conduct training and drills. Many agencies, in response to the national attention to school-based shootings, conduct "active shooter" training. This training occurs in the summer or on school vacations, when school buildings are empty. Officers, usually armed with paint ball guns, learn aggressive entry tactics, building search strategies and take-down techniques. In these training exercises, real people hide inside the school and play the role of actual shooters. These training sessions are useful to help officers learn entry strategies and best practices to locate and take down real threats. They are also beneficial because they familiarize officers with the physical layouts of the inside and outside of school property.

In addition to active shooter training, it is also necessary to conduct multi-agency, critical response drills. The first few drills should be done without teachers and students present in order to test response routes, radio communication, command posts, staging locations and other technicalities. The next step is a full school drill, conducted using all emergency responders and students and staff. It takes a lot of planning and resources, but is a necessary practice run to ensure that everyone understands her role. The importance of the post-incident meeting involving representatives from all agencies should not be overlooked. Problems should be identified and remedied so that all agencies can best respond in the future.

Building Safety and Security: Physical Tactics

Conducting active shooter training and critical incident drills is a reactive planning strategy. Administrators are literally planning to respond to a major incident. In an effort to prevent or reduce the likelihood of this type of event occurring, many schools have enacted proactive strategies through physical barriers and increased security measures on school property. Police officers who work with school districts can be a useful resource to conduct school security assessments and to make recommendations for improvements. Many schools have initiated a plan for controlled building access. This involves locking all doors to the school building except for one main entry door that is monitored. All visitors are required to pass through the main door and to then check in at the office. Other schools keep all the doors locked during school hours and have an outside buzzer that visitors must ring to gain entry. According to a 2007 Bureau of Justice survey, 85% of American schools use some form of controlled building access during schools hours *(DOJ, 2007, p. 59)*. Another popular method is the use of identification badges by school staff, students and visitors. The same survey revealed that 48% of schools in the study did require badges or picture ID for faculty and staff *(p. 59)*. The third most common strategy employed in American schools is the use of surveillance cameras. The survey found that 43% of the schools reported using cameras *(p. 59)*. Other strategies include: Use of a metal detector at school entrances; using dogs to check lockers for drugs or explosives; random sweeps for contraband and school uniforms.

Special Assignments: Officers Working Inside Schools

While a police officer assigned as the school liaison is an important partnership, it is certainly not a full-time assignment and does little to establish personal relationships with students. In an effort to better connect students with police officers two major programs have become extremely popular over the past few decades.

The Drug Abuse Resistance Education (DARE) program was established in Los Angeles in 1983 by Police Chief Daryl F. Gates. It developed into a national association known as DARE America. Thousands of police departments nationwide have sent officers to this extensive training and have specialized units comprised of DARE officers that work within the schools on a full-time basis. According to DARE America and the U.S. Department of Justice, this program is in place in over 10,000 communities and in over 300,000 classrooms across the country (www.dare-america.com).

Because of the extensive growth and popularity of the DARE program, it has been scrutinized and studied by researchers. The research is clear; DARE doesn't work to reduce drug or alcohol use. The conclusion of an extensive five year longitudinal study indicates that DARE graduates showed "…limited effects of the program upon drug use, greater efficacy with respect to attitudes, social skills, and knowledge, but a general tendency for curriculum effects to decay over time" *(Clayton, et al., 1996).*

Despite the consistent research findings that highlight DARE's failures, the program continues to be incredibly popular. This may be based on the statistically unsupported national attachment to the DARE concept. The fact is, DARE is a warm and fuzzy program and parents and students seem to support it. DARE officers can certainly contribute to positive police-community relationships with students, school staff and parents. Young adults may remember their DARE officer fondly and may feel more comfortable approaching police in general due to their positive experience with their school's DARE officer.

Another popular full-time assignment for police officers is working as a School Resource Officer (SRO). The SRO program has been around for years, but gained momentum in the 1990s. These officers are assigned to local schools, usually at the middle and high school levels. They can often be seen walking through the hallways, sitting at lunch talking with students, attending school sports functions and attending school meetings. Much like the DARE officer, SROs create and maintain positive community contacts with students. In addition, they are usually called upon to respond to incidents that occur within the school. They are often better equipped to handle these incidents when compared to general patrol officers. This is due to their knowledge of student social networks and understanding of school policies and procedures. A 2003 study found that 43% of police departments have full-time School Resource Officers and together they have 14,337 officers working in that capacity *(DOJ, 2006, p. 20, Table 43).*

Another important function of police officers who are assigned to work in the school system full-time is the early recognition and intervention of brewing problems. The DARE officer or School Resource Officer may be the first to recognize early signs of depression and suicidal thoughts, domestic violence in the home, alcohol and drug abuse, bullying and the presence of gangs inside the schools *(Special Focus 12.1)*. Early intervention can be of great benefit to individuals who are struggling with these issues and to those around them who could be adversely affected by future violent behavior.

With the recent economic downturn and continued budget cuts, many Chiefs have been forced to cut these positions. Both DARE officers and SROs have been taken out of the schools and have been re-assigned to the street to work as patrol officers. This is an unfortunate outcome of the economy, but police administrators can still ensure that the police remain a presence in schools by requiring consistent walkthroughs. The Park and Walk program, as discussed in previous chapters, is a great way to maintain a police presence inside schools. This program strengthens existing police-school partnerships and improves building familiarization.

Special Focus 12.1: Bullying

Over the past decade there has been growing concern over bullying in the nation's school systems. The prevalence of bullying, its potential link to homicidal and suicidal behavior, the early warning signs and the best methods to reduce bullying are all issues that are being evaluated by school and police personnel.

One commonly used definition of bullying can be found in a 1993 book written by Dr. Dan Olweus, a prominent researcher in this field of study. He postulated that bullying includes three essential elements: (1) the behavior is aggressive and negative; (2) the behavior is carried out repeatedly; and (3) the behavior occurs in a relationship where there is an imbalance of power between the parties involved (1993).

Bullying behavior can take many forms. Olweus identified both indirect and direct bullying. Indirect bullying refers to non-physical contact such as teasing, social ostracism and spreading gossip. Direct bulling involves physical contact such as pushing, slapping, punching, pinching or any other forms of physical violence (1993). Both boys and girls engage in bullying behavior. Boys are more likely to engage in direct bullying, while girls are more likely to engage in indirect bullying. Both forms are extremely damaging to the victim, especially if the behavior occurs continuously over a long period of time.

Bullying behavior occurs in schools nationwide. A survey found that in 2001, 14 percent of students ages 12 through 18 reported that they had been bullied at school in the 6 months prior to the interview (DOE, 2005). Gender differences were not detected in the survey, as both boys and girls experienced bullying at about the same rate (2005). Also, there were no differences measured between students who attended public or private schools (2005).

Can a police department have any effect on bullying behavior? Interestingly, the same survey revealed that lower rates of bullying were reported in schools that had police officers, security or staff hallway monitors (2005).

Some people may think back to their own school yard experiences and may recall involvement in bullying behavior either as the perpetrator or the victim. They may consider it a normal or common activity that does not deserve the public attention that it has received over the past decade. However, there is more to bullying than meets the eye and the long-term effects and connection to violent behavior have been strongly linked. In a study conducted by the U.S. Secret Service regarding school shootings, researchers wrote that, "In a number of cases, bullying placed a key role in the decision to attack. A number of attackers had experienced bullying and harassment that were longstanding and severe. In those cases, bullying appeared to play a major role in motivating the attack at the school" (USSS, 2002, p. 14).

Beyond school shootings, victims of bullying may experience a number of long-term effects. Victims suffer from depression, loneliness, anxiety, low self-esteem and even an increased susceptibility to illness. Studies have also linked the victims of bullying to poor academic performance when compared to non-bullied students (DOE, 2005). Recently, researchers have begun to study the link between being bullied and suicide.

On April 6, 2009, eleven-year-old Carl Joseph Walker-Hoover committed suicide by hanging himself with an

123

extension cord at his aunt's house in Springfield, Massachusetts (Plaisance, 2009). He had been a sixth grader at the New Leadership Charter School. After his death his mother, Sirdeaner L. Walker, talked openly about problems that her son was having at school. She told the media that in an effort to stop the bullying that her son was enduring she had repeatedly contacted school administrators beginning in September to report the behavior. She claimed that other students had been calling him gay, had made fun of the way he dressed and had threatened him on multiple occasions. In the end, it is her belief that chronic bullying at school was the direct cause of her son's death and that it could have been prevented if the school had been more responsive to her concerns.

The significant impact that bullying can have on an individual, and on that individual's surrounding community, cannot be overlooked. It is the responsibility of both school administrators and police personnel to create an effective system to prevent or reduce bullying behavior through early identification and response and through staff and student education.

Sources:

Olweus, D. (1993). *Bullying at School: What We Know and What We Can Do.* Cambridge, MA: Blackwell.

Plaisance, M., & Johnson, P. (2009, April 8). Mom says Springfield boy, 11, was repeatedly bullied at school. *The Republican,* p. A1.

U.S. Department of Education (DOE), National Center for Education Statistics. (2005). *Student Reports of Bullying: Results from the 2001 school crime supplement to the National Crime Victimization Survey.* NCES 2005-310. Washington, DC: U.S. Government Printing Office.

U. S. Secret Service (USSS), National Threat Assessment Center. (2002). Preventing school shootings: A summary of a U.S. Secret Service safe schools initiative report. *National Institute of Justice Journal,* 248, 14.

Educational Programming: Prevention through Understanding

Another proactive effort to include in any school-based planning strategy is the use of educational programming inside the schools. Teachers are often seeking guest speakers to discuss topics such as drunk driving, drug and alcohol use, sexual assault or family violence. Police officers should extend themselves as an available resource. Officers working in a teaching capacity benefit both the students and the officers who may enjoy the opportunity to engage in a new and challenging task.

In addition to conducting lectures for students, officers may also be invited to conduct training for teachers and staff members at a school. This training could include topics such as recognition of drugs, gang information, bullying, internet and computer safety, critical incident response or familiarization with departmental policies and laws.

Regardless of the program that is in place, school-police collaboration has many benefits. Having open lines of communication will lead to more effective and efficient response to incidents. The assignment of officers to work inside schools will help department members solve crimes by tapping into the officer's vast knowledge of social networks and individual activities. It will also provide an early intervention system to identify issues that may lead to violent behavior. Increasing police presence in schools will naturally increase individual interactions with officers and will contribute to an overall improved public image through positive community contacts.

Proven Success

The strategies that school and police administrators have been using, in combination with other community programs aimed at youth, are working. All involved should be hopeful for the future of safety within the nation's schools. This is important to recognize, as communities struggle to deal with the onslaught of major issues in schools including bullying, drug and alcohol use, physical violence, weapon possession and even terrorist attack. However, studies show improvement in many of these areas.

One self-reporting survey revealed decreases in drug and alcohol use by American students. A Pride Survey indicated that 58.3% of students reported using alcohol during the 1996 – 1997 school year, compared with 43.5% during the 2006 – 2007 school year *(2008)*. Over the same ten year period, the use of illicit drugs dropped from 30.1% to 19.2% *(2008)*. The study further identified specific drugs including marijuana, cocaine, uppers, downers, inhalants, hallucinogens, heroin, steroids, ecstasy, OxyContin and crystal methamphetamine. Every single category indicated a reduction in the use of these drugs over the ten-year assessment period *(2008)*.

Further research has focused on fear, both in the minds of students and parents. The Gallup Poll measured parents' attitudes over an eleven-year period, spanning from 1998 to 2009. Respondents were asked if they fear for their child's safety when they are at school. In 1998, 37% of parents reported that they did fear for their child's safety. This concern peaked in the post-Columbine month of May, 1999 at 52% *(2009)*. Since that time parental concern has dropped to 26% in 2009 *(2009)*.

Studies have also measured student concerns. Students were polled regarding their fear of attack at school or going to and from school. In 1995, 11.8% indicated that they were fearful, compared with 6.2% in 2005 *(DOJ, 2007)*. This change in perception may be related to successful administrative strategies on behalf of schools and police departments, or it could be a simple reflection of attention turned away from school-place issues and instead on war and the economy. In a study that is conducted yearly, citizens are asked to identify the biggest problems facing public schools. Interestingly, from 1988 through 1992, use of drugs/dope consistently ranked number one. Between 1993 – 2001, the biggest problem identified fluctuated between lack of funding, lack of discipline and fight/gang violence. From 2002 – 2008 however, lack of funding was rated as the biggest issue facing schools *(Gallup, 2008)*. The results of this longitudinal study are reflective of a new focus of concern.

All of these studies demonstrate a general trend in schools: things are getting better. These improvements are reported decades into the national transition into the Community Policing Era and beyond. While there are certainly many factors that have contributed to these improvements, police officers collaborating with school administrators have certainly been a strong contributor. It is for this reason that police agencies continue to build and maintain partnerships with school personnel.

Collaboration is a critical piece of any successful preventative and proactive police-school strategy. These partnerships can work to reduce drug and alcohol use, combat interpersonal violence, reduce intimidation and bullying behavior, improve police-public image and will provide unique and creative positions for officers who have the right skills and motivation to work in a school environment.

End Notes

Clayton, R., Cattarello, A., & Johnstone, B. (1996, May). The Effectiveness of DARE: 5-year follow-up results. *Preventive Medicine,* 25(3), 307 – 318.

DARE America. Mission. Retrieved September 20, 2009, from http://www.dare-america.com/home/InsideDAREAmerica/ Story43fd.asp?N=InsideDARE America&S=13&S=28

Gallup, G. Jr. (2008). *The Gallup Report,* Report Nos. 276 & 288. Princeton, NJ: The Gallup Poll.

The Gallup Organization, Inc., *The Gallup Poll* (2009) [Online]. Retrieved May 29, 2009 from: http://www.gallup.com/poll/ 1588/Children-Violence.aspx

Olweus, D. (1993). *Bullying at School: What We Know and What We Can Do.* Cambridge, MA: Blackwell.

Plaisance, M., & Johnson, P. (2009, April 8). Mom says Springfield boy, 11, was repeatedly bullied at school. *The Republican,* p. A1.

PRIDE Surveys. (2008). *2006 – 2007 PRIDE Surveys National Summary, Grades 6 through 12.* Bowling Green, KY: PRIDE Surveys, 288 – 289.

U.S. Department of Education (DOE), National Center for Education Statistics. (2005). *Student Reports of Bullying: Results from the 2001 school crime supplement to the National Crime Victimization Survey.* NCES 2005-310. Washington, DC: U.S. Government Printing Office.

U.S. Department of Justice (DOJ), Bureau of Justice Statistics. (2006, May). *Local police departments, 2003.* NCJ 210118. Washington, DC: U.S. Government Printing Office.

U.S. Department of Justice (DOJ), Office of Justice Programs. (2007, December). *Indicators of School Crime and Safety: 2007.* NCJ 219553. Washington, DC: U.S. Government Printing Office.

U. S. Secret Service (USSS), National Threat Assessment Center. (2002). Preventing school shootings: A summary of a U.S. Secret Service safe schools initiative report. *National Institute of Justice Journal,* 248, 14.

Although the daily duties of a police officer are strikingly similar to what they were forty years ago, there have also been dramatic improvements and changes that have affected the work environment. There have been incredible developments in computer technology, management and leadership theory, patrol tactics, equipment, vehicles and communications. Along with these varied advancements, the social and political climates have also transformed. Most people, including working police officers, would agree that these changes have been positive and that police departments today are more efficient, more professional and are better able to respond to a wider variety of situations than in years past. Despite this acknowledgment of positive change and improvement, it does nothing to prevent the natural human tendency to resist change.

Most individuals feel safer and more comfortable in familiar and consistent environments. Altering those environments can breed fear, anxiety, self-doubt and a general feeling of losing control. Many sociological and psychological models of change have gone so far as to compare the change experience with the grieving process. In her book, *On Death and Dying,* Elizabeth Kubler-Ross developed a theory that identified the specific emotional steps in the grieving process including shock, denial, blame, anger, uncertainty and finally acceptance and action planning *(1969).* This parallel of comparing death to changes in the workplace may seem over dramatic, but people spend forty or more hours a week at their jobs. Often, they see coworkers more than they see their own families. The workplace is a very significant portion of someone's life and changes to that can have a major impact.

A History of Resisting Change

This innate resistance to change is particularly well entrenched in the firmly established history of policing *(Guyet, 1979)*. This point is strongly illustrated by the attempted implementation, and ultimate rejection, of team policing in the 1970s *(Sherman, Milton, & Kelly, 1973)*. Resistance to change in policing can be seen occurring again and again through time, across different agencies and involving minor and major changes. Officers from a small city police department expressed their dislike for new accreditation stickers that were affixed to some of the patrol cruisers. Administrators had placed the stickers there to highlight the department's hard-earned accomplishment. Some officers who had actively vocalized their disdain for accreditation refused to drive the cars with accreditation stickers on them. This example illustrates how resistant some people are. Even an obviously positive (and minor) change resulted in friction and tension between the officers and the administration.

Successfully Implementing Change

So often change is forced on personnel by administrators. Chiefs implement the change and officers immediately react and work against it. Two groups form, metaphorically pushing against each other and causing frustration, anger, distrust and low morale. Ideally, all personnel would be in the same group, moving forward together to accomplish the change. But how can an administrator get everyone on board to work toward change?

Accept that Change Is Inevitable

First, accept and convey that change is inevitable. Truthfully, it should be viewed as a constant and a sign of a progressive agency. The world changes quickly and public and private sector managers must do their best to keep up with advances and improvements in their respective fields. The best leaders will not resist change but will embrace it, expect it and even seek it. Recognition and acceptance of the need for improvement and change and viewing it positively is critical. It is also important to understand the difficulty that employees experiencing change will go through and to work to ease this process. There are specific strategies that can be used to make a transition easier.

Give Advanced Warning

It is of the greatest importance that those who will be affected by the change receive advance warning. This will give everyone time to understand why the change is being made, how the change is being made and perhaps to embrace it. Giving people time to process and consider the proposal will greatly increase acceptance.

Explain the Reason for the Change

All personnel must understand why the change is being implemented. Many changes have obvious advantages but highlighting those benefits and connecting them to the individual is an effective way to work toward acceptance. One issue that always seems to draw great resistance is changes in computer software. Many agencies have made the transition from the combination typewriter and Polaroid system to police-specific software that incorporates digital images. The updated software, such as the popular IMC program, is much more efficient, user-friendly and organized. It also allows for easier review of calls for service, crime statistics and general departmental activity. It is a better way to document the varied tasks that police officers do throughout their days. Despite these over-whelming benefits many officers who had been using the old system and who had some level of technophobia within them expressed great resistance. However, with ample warning and clear articulation of the many advantages of the new software, people were slowly able to accept it.

Involve Employees in the Change Process

Another important step, and one so often overlooked by managers, is the need to involve the entire agency in the change process. Seeking input and asking for suggestions and guidance will empower employees and will make them more likely to accept the change because they may view it as their own idea or initiative. It is wise to create a smaller group of employees whose function is to determine how to best implement the change. Members of this group should be the agency's informal leaders and not necessarily the formal managers. As discussed earlier in this book, natural leaders can be easily identified among the rank and file. Formal managers may have a stripe on their arm or a bar on their shoulder but in order to get personnel to work toward change, they need to see the agency's natural leaders supporting it.

Once a working group has been established, all personnel should be kept in the loop regarding the change. Updates on anticipated dates of implementation or modifications to the original idea should be conveyed to all. Many departments have added new less than lethal force options, such as taser guns, to their arsenal of weapons. Some officers may support the use of tasers and some may not feel comfortable with them. The working group should be responsible for thoroughly researching the item and should keep the staff apprised of developments in this area. Communication is critical before, during and after the change.

Using this technique of a working group and free-flowing communication supports the theory that change should be introduced gradually. Everyone needs time to adjust and slow and steady change will be much more effective and likely to stick than a sudden directive that seems out of left field.

Provide Orientation and Training (if necessary)

Specific types of change, particularly related to technology, will require ample orientation and training. Everyone needs to have a working understanding of the new policy, software or equipment. If adequate training is not given, personnel will quickly become frustrated and the new piece of equipment will not be used or the policy will not be adhered to. This is particularly true when a department is installing new computer software or is upgrading existing technology. It is worth spending the extra money and time to invest in training so that everyone feels as comfortable as possible. Investing in preparing personnel is an important step in success and acceptance of change.

Prepare to Reassess and Improve

Finally, all involved should be ready to make adjustments and improvements to the original concept. Administrators should encourage open communication and should strive to accept feedback and use it to make improvements. Those people working most directly with the change will have the most valuable opinions and they should be encouraged to give them. Similar to using the SARA method to problem solve as community police officers, this same model can and should be applied to issues within an agency. The SARA model is an agent for change and one of the most important step in that model is the final assessment phase. The assessment phase is in place because it is impossible to predict all angles. The implementation of a program often reveals things that had not been previously considered. Administrators should not interpret alterations as a failure but rather be open to flexibility and improvement even after the change has been implemented.

Not every single change in an agency requires establishing change groups and gradual implementation. Minor improvements, such as new forms, a simple policy change or the attainment of a familiar piece of equipment will not require much fanfare. Before implementing any change, administrators should consider the gravity of the proposal and how it will affect each employee. Those recommendations that will have a significant impact on the workforce should be handled thoughtfully.

The most important piece of any change is planning. But this should not be limited to the change itself and how the new policy will work. Instead, planning should focus on both the change and the successful implementation of that change by preparing affected employees for the transition. Poor planning and overlooking the impact that the change will have on personnel may lead to rejection, failure and frustration.

As history has proven, change is often good. The state of policing is better today than it was decades ago. Agencies are more professional, more efficient, better able to understand and meet the needs of citizens and officers are able to perform a wider variety of tasks. These improvements have come through changes, painstakingly navigated by police supervisors over the past few decades. Change is constant. It is not something to be feared or resisted. Many people would agree that it is often not the actual change that is the issue. Instead, it is the way that it was implemented. With this in mind supervisors and administrators can focus on understanding the best practice for making change and can use that model as a guide.

Conclusion

This book has provided an overview of the state of policing today. It was designed to act as a guide for police supervisors and administrators who are facing the continual challenges of leading today's law enforcement agencies. It examines many aspects of a police agency and identifies specific and practical steps that police leaders can put into practice. The majority of these strategies require little, if any, financial resources. Instead, they require augmenting current daily tasks with new responsibilities and sometimes modifying the way in which officers currently perform their jobs.

All of these strategies push agencies to continue on with existing programs and to explore new ones. They work to meet the many goals that were identified earlier in this book, including working proactively to reduce crime, improving the overall quality of life in a community, building and maintaining citizen relationships and support and providing a workplace for officers that fosters pride, increases morale and improves retention.

Police managers today are in a new era. They are facing increasing challenges that must be met to keep their communities safe, while also struggling to attract, hire and supervise the new generation of Millennial police officers. These challenges are not easy. But, with an understanding of the state of policing today and of the many new and effective strategies that are available, police managers can move forward with confidence and diligence.

End Notes

Guyet, D. (1979). Bending Granite: Attempts to change the rank and structure of American police departments. *Journal of Police Sciences and Administration,* 7(3), 253 – 284.

Kubler-Ross, E. (1969). *On Death and Dying.* New York: MacMillan.

Sherman, L. W., Milton, C. H., & Kelly, T. V. (1973). *Team Policing: Seven case studies.* Washington DC: Police Foundation.

Academy training 83
Accountability 100
Accreditation 73, 74
Accreditation process 75
Active shooter training 119
Administrative duties 71, 72
Ask a Cop Programs 95
Axis of evil 8
Bicycle patrol 104
Broken Windows article 7
Broken Windows theory 16
Brown, Lee 20
Bullying 122
Change
    implementing 130
    reason for; explain 131
    resisting 130
Citizen Police Academy (CPA) 107
Citizen survey 114
College-educated officers 78
Columbine High School 117
Columbine incident 117
Commission on Accreditation for Law Enforcement Agencies,
    Inc. (CALEA®) 73
Community Oriented Policing Services (COPS) 8
Community outreach 107
Community partnerships through collaboration 100
Community policing .... iii, 11, 58
    defined 12
    identifying the problems 19
    key elements of 14
Community Policing Era 7, 17, 23, 31, 97
Community Services Bureau (CSB) 25
Critical response drills 119
Cruiser patrol 103
Department of Justice 24

Dilbert Principle 65
Drug Abuse Resistance Education (DARE) 120
Early policing history 1
Educational programming 125
Educational programming inside schools 125
Foot patrol 104
Formal commendation 85
Generation Y 49
Goldstein, Herman 7
Homeland security 31
    department of 32
Implementing change 130
In-house classes 82
Incident training and drills 119
Informal feedback 85
Interns 113
Interoperability 32
Kansas City Preventative Patrol Experiment (KCPPE) 6
Kelling, George 7
King, Rodney 91
Leadership styles 57
London Metropolitan Police 1
Management by Walking Around 60
Manager v. Leader 57
Media 34, 91
Media coverage; generating positive 93
Media materials; creating 95
Media relations 91
    working relationships 92
Memorandum of Understanding (MOU) 118
Millennial Generation 49
Minimum hiring standards 76
Mission Statements 37
    sample 37
Neighborhood Watch 111
Neighborhood Watch orientation 111
Online training 82
Park and Walk 110, 122
Park and walk programs 105

Patrol assignment; geographic 99
Patrol operations 103
Peel, Robert 1
Peel's Principles 2
Performance evaluations 67
Personnel evaluations 84
Peter Principle 64
Police Community Relations (PCR) 5
Police image, contributions to 95
Police training 82
Police Website 94
Police Week or Police Day 113
Political Era 3
Positive public image 41
Post-incident meeting 119
Pride Survey 126
Proactive approach 97
Public service announcements 95
Quality of life issues 39
Rape Aggression Defense (RAD) 113
Recruiting strategies 43
Recruitment 42
Recruitment and hiring 80
Reengineering the corporation 59
Reform Era 4
Resisting change 130
Ride-along programs 110
Robert Half International Survey 54
Robert Peel 1
   Principles of Law Enforcement 2
Rodney King 91
SARA 7, 98, 133
School Resource Officer (SRO) 121
School safety 105, 117
School-police union 119
Self-defense programs 113
Self-initiated activity 68
Sexual Assault Response Team (SART) 101
Sheriff's Theft Offense Prosecution Program (STOPP) 98

Sick time use 67
Team policing 130
Technology 33, 34, 86
Terrorism 32
Total quality management 60
Total Quality Management (TQM) 60, 62
Wilson, James Q. 7

Path of the Warrior - *2nd Edition*
   An Ethical Guide to Personal & Professional
      Development in the Field of Criminal Justice
by Larry F. Jetmore

The COMPSTAT Paradigm
   Management Accountability in Policing,
      Business and the Public Sector
by Vincent E. Henry, CPP, Ph.D.

The New Age of Police Supervision and Management
   A Behavioral Concept
by Michael A. Petrillo & Daniel R. DelBagno

Handgun Combatives - *2nd Edition*
by Dave Spaulding

Advanced Vehicle Stop Tactics
   Skills for Today's Survival Conscious Officer
by Michael T. Rayburn

Advanced Patrol Tactics
   Skills for Today's Street Cop
by Michael T. Rayburn

Anatomy of a Motor Vehicle Stop
   Essentials of Safe Traffic Enforcement
by Det. Joseph Petrocelli and Matthew Petrocelli, Ph.D.

Developing the Survival Attitude
   A Guide for the New Officer
by Phil L. Duran

Tactical Attitude
   Learn from Powerful Real-Life Experience!
   Includes *Officer Survival Creed* (Suitable for framing)
by Phil L. Duran & Dennis Nasci

How to Really, *Really* Write Those Boring Police
Reports
by Kimberly Clark

(800) 647-5547   www.LooseleafLaw.com